WATER OF LIFE

an all-age three-year teaching and worship programme

sermon illustrations

kevin mayhew

First published in 2006 by

KEVIN MAYHEW LTD
Buxhall, Stowmarket, Suffolk, IP14 3BW
E-mail: info@kevinmayhewltd.com
Web: www.kevinmayhew.com

Sermon Illustrations is extracted from
Waters of Life – Complete Resource Book

9 8 7 6 5 4 3 2 1 0

ISBN 1 84417 596 0
Catalogue No 1500910

Cover design by Sara-Jane Came
Compiled by Peter Dainty
Edited and typeset by Katherine Laidler

Printed in Great Britain

Contents

Introduction

This booklet brings together the weekly Thoughts for the Day and Illustrations from the *Complete Resource Book* in a handy form for the use of the preacher or worship leader in preparation for, and during, the church service.

The Thought for the Day is meant to touch the heart and the will as well as the mind. If you are using it as the basis of your message during the service, do spend a good deal of time with it the week before. Use the Illustration to reinforce it and relate the topic to the lives and experience of the congregation. Remember that a story, a poem or a visual image can say much more than dull prose. Remember also that the Thought for the Day is meant to lead to some sort of action or reaction.

DAVID ADAM

THE LORD OUR GOD
Ever-present Creator

Aim

To show that Jesus Christ was with the Father before the foundation of the world.

Readings

Proverbs 8:1, 22-31
Psalm 104:24; 139:1-12
Colossians 1:15-20
John 1:1-14

Thought for the day

Today's readings are telling us that Jesus was there before the creation of the world and working with the Father. John's Gospel starts with the same words as Genesis: 'In the beginning'. Genesis says, 'In the beginning God . . .' and John says, 'In the beginning was the Word, and the Word was with God, and the Word was God.' Not only was Jesus present but Jesus shared in the creation: 'all things came into being through him . . . in him was life and the life was the light of men' (John 1:3-4).

Not only was Christ there, but we are actually in him. All creation is in him, as it is in the Father and the Holy Spirit. Paul in Colossians says of Christ, 'In him all things in heaven and on earth were created.' This is a great mystery, which we will never fully understand with our minds, but we can know it with our hearts. We need to rejoice in God and need to know in our hearts that we are never outside of him.

Illustration

There is a fountain in India with fish around it. On the fountain are words by the Indian poet Kabir: 'I laugh if I hear the fish in the sea are thirsty. I laugh if I hear man goes in search of God.'

Just think of a little fish living in a mighty ocean being told its whole life depends on water. One morning it sets out to find water. It leaves its home and travels to cold seas but it cannot find water there. It then travels south to warmer climes, still seeking, but it cannot see water there. It searches all of the seas and all this time it is restless and weary, spending much of its energy. At last it meets an old fish on the seabed and asks, 'Where is the water for I would like some?' 'Do you not know you live in the water, you move in the water, you only exist because of the water? There is no need to look for it, you are in it. If you did not have it you would die. Enjoy being in it; know that it is all around you.' This was wonderful news; there was no need to seek but there was a chance to enjoy the element in which it lived.

St Paul, when he was speaking about God to the Greeks on the Areopagus, says, 'In him we live and move and have our being' (Acts 17:28). This is a wonderful reality to discover: we need not seek God for we are in God, in his presence and in his love. Let us enjoy this reality.

God's Voice

Aim

To learn the importance of listening to God.

Readings

1 Samuel 3:1-10
Psalm 95
Hebrews 3:12–4:2; 4:11-13
Mark 4:1-9

Thought for the day

The story of Samuel at Shiloh illustrates how the Church must often appear. Eli represents the Church; he is old and losing his vision. The light in the church has almost gone out. The sons of the 'vicarage', Hophni and Phineas, are not interested in following in their father's footsteps. Into this situation is introduced a youngster and, as ever, he disturbs the church. Eli is trying to sleep. Samuel lies on his mattress listening to the sounds of the night. A voice calls. Samuel, who is about 12 years old, jumps up and wakes the old man Eli and says, 'You called.' Tired, Eli says, 'I did not call. Go back to bed, my son.' The Lord calls again, 'Samuel!' Once more Samuel jumps up and runs to Eli because he doesn't know it was the Lord who was calling. Again Eli says, 'I did not call. Go back to bed, my son.' It is not long before the Lord calls a third time. For a third time Samuel disturbs Eli. This old priest, his vision fading, is able to guide the young man and send him back to his room, saying, 'If he calls, you shall say, "Speak, Lord, for your servant is listening."'

The Church might be very old and find the young disturbing, but God speaks through new voices. At the same time the young will be lost without the guidance of the old.

Samuel heard the voice and said, 'Speak, Lord, for your servant is listening.' In this way God was able to speak to Samuel and *through* Samuel.

Jesus compares the preacher to a sower who scatters his seed in different soils. As the good soil receives the seed, so the good listener receives the word and allows it to bear fruit.

Illustration

Hello!
Are you receiving me?
Hello!
Are you receiving me?
Hello!
Are you receiving me?

This was a conversation, if you can call it that, on a mobile phone. The person was in a bad reception area. There was too much interference from hills and trees. They would have to go to a better reception area.

It is amazing how many people and nations are good at speaking but find it very hard to hear anyone. Our speakers (mouths) seem to be far more active than our receivers (ears). A proverb from the East says, 'God gave us two ears and one mouth so that we should listen twice as much as we speak.'

Committed to God

Aim

To affirm our commitment to Christ.

Readings

Joshua 24:1-2a, 14-18
Psalm 34:15-22
Ephesians 6:10-20
John 6:56-69

Thought for the day

God does not force himself upon us. He has given us the freedom to choose whether we serve him or not. He gives himself to us in love and we can choose whether to return that love or to ignore him. Some definitely choose to ignore or go against God; others ignore him by default – that is, they let other things and people squeeze God out. If we are to love and serve God, we have to be sure we have made this a definite choice.

Joshua called the tribes of Israel together and asked them to dedicate their lives to the true God. If they were unwilling to serve the Lord, they should at least choose whom they were going to serve, whether it was the gods of Egypt or the gods of the Amorites. There is always the danger of not making a clear choice. Joshua gave a lead by saying, 'As for me and my household, we will serve the LORD.'

Once they were given a lead, the Israelites declared they would not desert the LORD and follow other gods. They then recited how the LORD delivered them from Egypt and from slavery: the LORD did great wonders in their sight and the LORD protected them. 'Therefore we will also serve the LORD for he is our God.' The Israelites made a definite decision to serve the LORD.

In today's Gospel we find two definite groups of people. Those who find the teaching too hard, who take offence and do not believe, belong to the first group. They turn away from Jesus and no longer go with him. There are many who do this. The second group are those who seek to stay with him and be loyal to him. Amongst those are the disciples. Jesus asks them, 'Do you also wish to go away?' They are not forced to stay: if they want, they can leave. Judas will later prove the possibility of this. Simon Peter replies for the disciples and says, 'Lord, to whom can we go? You have the words of eternal life. We have come to believe and know that you are the Holy One of God.'

We are given the opportunity of turning away from him or committing ourselves to follow him. This is not just a one-off choice; we have to make it every day and sometimes many times in a day.

Illustration

Here is a story of loyalty. A man and his dog walked in the hill country. The man saw an old mine in a hillside and went in. Whilst inside, the roof collapsed and trapped the man by his leg. For a while the dog stayed with him but it then went outside the mine and stood at the entrance. There it began to howl to attract attention. No one took any notice at first. The dog became hungry and thirsty but it did not leave its post. The weather became bad; the dog got wet and cold but it stayed put and continued to howl. Finally a nearby farmer decided there was something wrong with the dog and he climbed the hillside to find it. When he arrived, the dog stopped howling but would not let him touch it or even feed it. It tried to lead him into the mine. The farmer made to go away but as soon as he did this the dog started to howl and to walk towards the mine again. At last he decided to go to the entrance and call to see if there was anyone there. He heard a voice and so went cautiously inside. He saw the man was trapped and went for help. The dog seemed to understand because it now stayed with its master and remained with him until help came and he was rescued.

God's Growing Kingdom

Aim

To show that the kingdom of God is waiting to grow in us.

Readings

Ezekiel 17:22-24
Psalm 65
1 Corinthians 3:1-9
Mark 4:26-34

Thought for the day

The Church is in the growth business. We are called to sow seeds and to encourage growth. Today's Gospel has two of the parables of Jesus about the kingdom of God and growth.

'The kingdom of God is as if someone would scatter seed.' There has to be a sowing: the Church must proclaim the message. We may often feel we have failed but we need to have patience and to trust in God. The seed must be given time to germinate. Once the sowing is done, the farmer gets on with other things, including other sowings. While he sleeps and does other things the seed starts to grow – remember it can only do this if it was sown in the first place.

'The earth produces of itself'; it does this automatically for that is what the Greek word means. We do not create the kingdom. We can prepare for its growth in us and in others, but God gives the increase. Growth is often imperceptible, sometimes slow; sometimes it takes much patience. But if we sow, we should trust that God is at work. There will be a harvest – that is, if you have sown the seeds.

(Show a mustard seed.) Most of you will not be able to see this because it is so tiny. In fact, I must be careful I do not lose it. It is a mustard seed. When talking of something small, the people who lived in the Holy Land would say, 'as small as a mustard seed' because it was the smallest of things. Yet in our amazing world, packed into this tiny seed is a large shrub. In the Holy Land it grows to something that looks like a tree, nearly two and a half metres high. Often you see birds sitting in its branches picking off the little black seeds. This is a wonderful thing if you think about it. God's kingdom is also amazing in the way it grows. Again, we have to do the sowing but God will give the increase.

To the early Church which was often facing opposition and setbacks, like the Church now, these were parables of encouragement. Sow the seed and trust God. The faith spread, the Church grew, the kingdom increased against opposition and persecution. This happened because the early Christians continued to sow the word of God in the hearts of people and the society in which they lived.

Illustration

Jonathan Chapman used to travel around farms in America with his Bible. In the evenings he would read to the family; not many of them could read themselves. They looked forward to his visits and they called him 'Johnny Appleseed'.

This is how he got his nickname. On some farms he noticed the men busy making cider. The apples were pressed and when the juice was extracted the pips were thrown away. 'What a waste,' thought Johnny: those little pips could grow into fine trees. So Johnny asked if he could have some seed. The man replied he could have as much seed as he wanted. Johnny filled his saddlebag with seeds. When he visited a farm, in the evening he read from the Bible, then before he left he would make some holes in the soil and plant some apple seeds. He then made a little fence around them to protect them and to give them the chance to grow. For over 40 years Johnny did this work, sowing the word of God in the hearts of people and sowing apple seeds in the ground. Everywhere he went he left something behind to give pleasure and nourishment to the farming people. He understood well that seeds could not grow unless they were planted.

God with Us

Aim

To know that whatever happens in this world or to us, God is always with us and promises us the victory through Jesus Christ our Lord.

Readings

Daniel 12:1-3
Psalm 16
Hebrews 10:11-14 (15-18) 19-25
Mark 13:1-8

Thought for the day

The dark cold days will soon be here. It will be as if darkness is triumphing over light. It is a time when people easily despair. So often the news of world events or what is happening nearer home does nothing to uplift us. We need to hear the Good News, we need to know that Christ is risen, that God is in control and that life is eternal.

Today's Gospel hardly sounds like Good News. As Jesus came out of the temple, the disciples admired the solidity and largeness of the stones and building. Surely the temple was a symbol of endeavour and lasting achievements. The temple, which Herod built, was one of the wonders of the world. It was begun in about 20 BC and was not completed when Jesus was alive. Josephus tells us that some of the stones were 40 feet long by 12 feet high and 18 feet wide. It was these stones that suggested strength and solidity to the disciples. Jesus, however, saw that they were not 'for ever'; in fact, he prophesied that the stones would all be thrown down and the temple destroyed. Salvation was not found in the temple.

In AD 70 Jerusalem fell after being under siege: over a million people died of starvation and the temple was destroyed. When the Gospel was written, Mark could have known this fact. This does not detract from the conversation of Jesus on the Mount of Olives; if anything, it enhances his prophecy.

It is too easy to trust in things we think will last when only God is eternal. All sorts will lead us astray promising us youth, fitness, peace, life: yet all these are dependent on God alone. False Christs abound, promising quick deliverance – beware. The world is in the grip of the evil one. There will be wars and rumours of wars, there will be famines. There will be all sorts of pain and suffering. You cannot escape them in this world. But these are only the beginning of the birth pangs of the new age, the new kingdom that is dawning. We may feel we are losing battle after battle (and this sadly can be true) but the final victory is assured us in Christ Jesus our Lord. Think again on the words from the hymn 'All my hope on God is founded':

> Human pride and earthly glory,
> sword and crown betray his trust;
> what with care and toil he buildeth,
> tower and temple fall to dust.
> But God's power, hour by hour,
> is my temple and my tower.

Our trust is not to be in any man-made thing, not even in the Church or prayer; our trust is to be in God alone. In the words of Julian of Norwich, 'He did not say, "You shall not be tempest-tossed, you shall not travail; you shall not be distressed." But he said, "You shall not be overcome."' It is this trust in God that made Julian to understand these words the Lord spoke to her:

> I shall make all things well.
> I may make all things well,
> and I can make all things well;
> and you shall see yourself that all things shall be well.

No matter how dark the days, the Light of Christ is with us: we are never alone or left in the dark. Victory is ours through him who loves us.

Illustration

When you go to an airport there are two places with frightening names. There is the 'departure lounge' and the 'terminal'. One is for those who are departing from us and the other is where it all ends! Well, you could look at it that way. Sometimes the departure lounge is a sad place because we are seeing people off whom we might not see again for a long time. But usually it is full of excited people who are going on holiday or going somewhere special. When we come to the terminal, it is not that we are going to stop there. It can be where all traffic is halted but we are going on to a better place. We are not going to stop at the terminal.

I tell you this because Jesus was talking about the end of the world, as we know it. He was pointing out that there are certain signs that point us towards what seems to be the end. But for us it is the beginning of something new. All the troubles are but the birth pangs of the coming of the kingdom. It is easy to quake with fear when we do not know what lies ahead. But we do know who is waiting to meet us. We may fear that we are losing round after round of the battle but in Christ Jesus we are assured the victory will be ours. The terminal will be where we move on to a better kingdom.

Loving God

Aim

To encourage love of God and of each other.

Readings

Deuteronomy 6:1-9
Psalm 119:1-8
1 John 4:7-21
Mark 12:28-34

Thought for the day

The opening scene is a typical one: religious authorities disputing with one another. So often the Church is seen in dispute with itself, talking about God rather than talking to him.

One of the scribes comes and asks Jesus which is the greatest commandment. The answer Jesus gives is the traditional Jewish answer: 'Hear, O Israel: the Lord your God is one; you shall love the Lord your God with all your heart, and with all your soul, and with all your mind, and with all your strength.' The emphasis is that there is only one God and that God asks us for our love. There is no conflict here: this is a Jewish student bringing a question to a teacher and receiving an answer. Jesus is quoting from Deuteronomy 6:4-5. This is known as the Shema, which is the imperative Hebrew word for 'hear' or 'listen'. So the whole gets its name from the first word. This hearing demands attention and obedience, two things we can often be weak on. It is with this sentence (Deuteronomy 6:4-5) that the service in the synagogue begins every day. 'You shall love the Lord your God' is part of the daily prayers for every Jew.

In this account by Mark, the words 'with all your mind' have been added to the original. As Mark's community contained many Gentiles, it was obviously felt important to offer the mind along with the rest of us. In fact, God wants us to offer our whole self to him in love.

These words were also contained in little leather boxes called phylacteries (Matthew 23:5), which the devout Jew strapped to his hand and his forehead when he was at prayer (Deuteronomy 6:8). In the same way the words were put into a little cylindrical box called the mezzuzah and fixed to every door of a Jewish house. It was to remind them that God was ever with them in their going out and coming in (Deuteronomy 6:9). These were words that they were to keep in their heart, recite to their children and talk about. It would do us well to know them and to practise what they say.

To this first commandment Jesus added another commandment: 'You shall love your neighbour as yourself.' This is a quotation from Leviticus (19:18b). The Jews were to love fellow Jews and allowed to hate Gentiles. Here with Jesus this love is to be all-inclusive and applies to everyone.

Jesus was the first to put these two commandments together and show how they were dependent on each other. St John will say:

> Whoever does not love does not know God, for God is love (1 John 4:8).
>
> God is love and those who abide in love abide in God and God abides in them (1 John 4:16b).
>
> Those who say, 'I love God', and hate their brothers or sisters, are liars; for those who do not love a brother or sister whom they have seen, cannot love God whom they have not seen (1 John 4:20).

Jesus makes these two commandments into one and shows how we cannot love God if we hate any of his creation, and we cannot truly learn to love our neighbours if we do not love God. Very often in this world the love of another human is the way to reveal to us the love of God.

Illustration

My Dearest,

I love you with all my heart.

I think of you every minute of the day.

I would do anything for you. I would swim shark-infested rivers to get to you. I would climb the steepest of mountains. I would travel the whole earth to be with you. I would brave fire and frost, wind and hail to be at your side.

But I cannot see you this week. I was coming tonight but it is too cold and damp for me to bother. Tomorrow I have fitness training and I am out with the lads the day after. I have a new computer game I want to try out on Wednesday, and a match to go to on Thursday. Friday as ever is swimming, and on Saturday the finals are on the television. I would do anything for you but it is a busy week. Sorry.

Keep in touch,
Yours always.

Not what I would call a promising relationship but is this the way we often deal with God and our prayers? Do we really love the Lord with all our heart?

GOD FEEDS US
The Bread of Life

Aim
To see Jesus as the Bread of Life.

Readings
Exodus 16:2-4, 9-15
Psalm 78:23-29
1 Timothy 4:1-8
John 6:24-35

Thought for the day
The early Church met regularly for the breaking of the bread. It is not surprising that there is a deep interest in Jesus as the Bread of Life. Today's Gospel ends with Jesus saying, 'I am the bread of life' (John 6:35).

It is worth looking at the questions raised in today's Gospel and the response Jesus gives to each of them as he seeks to clarify what true faith entails.

'Rabbi, when did you come here?' allows Jesus to discuss the motives of those who seek him: 'You are looking for me, not because you saw signs, but because you ate your fill of the loaves.' We often fail to read the signs that point us to God. We journey on, ever seeking, and ignore the God who can satisfy our emptiness and who is in our midst. We fill our lives with perishable goods and forget the One who alone gives eternal life. 'Do not work for the food that perishes, but for the food that endures to eternal life, which the Son of Man will give you.'

'What must we do to perform the works of God?' The work of God is to believe in him and in whom he has sent. The Greek word for 'believe' is far more than an assent to certain ideas about God; it is to have 'faith' in him: that is, to have a living relationship with God. Faith is about our personal relationship with the living God and with Jesus whom he has sent. If we do not have a relationship with God, we cannot truly perform his works. We are asked to give our heart to God. The German word 'belieben' is the root of the English word 'believe' and it means 'to belove'.

'What sign are you going to give us, then, so that we may believe in you? What work are you performing?' They hungered for more signs and more excitement and failed to seek the relationship that Jesus was offering. 'Our ancestors ate the manna in the wilderness; as it is written, "He gave them bread from heaven to eat."' Jesus responds by saying it was God not Moses that fed them in the wilderness and God gives you 'the true bread from heaven': that is, Jesus who came down from heaven and gives life to the world (John 6:33).

'Sir, give us this bread always.' The 'always' on this occasion is the Greek work 'pantote', which means again and again and again. Once more they have missed the point. Jesus clearly says, 'I am the bread of life. Whoever comes to me will never be hungry, and whoever believes in me will never be thirsty' (John 6:35). By saying, 'I am the bread of life', Jesus is saying he is linked to the 'I Am' who is God: he is God. The love of God is revealed in Jesus Christ and he meets the needs of those with inner hunger and thirst. In whatever situation we find ourselves we can trust in the unfailing power and love of God. There is no doubt that in writing his Gospel John was aware of the sacramental implications of the bread.

Illustration

Throughout our world there are people who seem to have to fill their lives with food, with things or with activity. No matter how much they get, they are still not satisfied. When young people say they are bored, it is usually when they have plenty happening around them but they recognise emptiness within. Bored means having a hole drilled in you. There is something in you that things cannot fill, no matter how you stuff yourself or your days. God made us for himself and nothing else will really fill the space he created within us for himself. In each of us there is a space for the eternal and nothing less than the eternal God can fill it.

Bread from Heaven

Aim

To show the calling of God and the stalling of our hearts.

Readings

1 Kings 19:4-8
Psalm 34:1-8
1 Corinthians 10:14-17
John 6:35, 41-51

Thought for the day

John's Gospel continues with the reactions of the people to the feeding of the five thousand. For John this is in the context of the Passover festival and of the Christian breaking of the bread meetings. The readings from John 6 obviously have a Eucharistic setting.

We begin today where last week's Gospel ended with Jesus saying, 'I am the bread of life.' Sadly the reaction of the people was to start 'murmuring', complaining about him (6:41). Jesus is offering himself to them and all they can do is grumble and complain. How often the great mystery of God's gift of himself to us is lost because of our attitude and prejudices. God has always worked through his creation and has come to us time and again through the ordinary, but we fail to see it because we are so prejudiced against it. We are forever looking for another miracle whilst God is actually offering himself to us. The people did not see that Jesus could be anyone special, and certainly thought he could not be God's Son, or the 'Bread of Life', because they knew where he lived. They refused to see beyond the obvious: that they thought they knew his mum and dad! Jesus tells them to stop murmuring, stop complaining and grumbling. The people with Moses had grumbled against him and therefore against God (Exodus 15:24; 16:2). It was believed that such grumbling prevented them coming into the Promised Land. 'Do not complain as some of them did, and were destroyed by the destroyer' (1 Corinthians 10:10). How often we miss out on the mystery and wonder of God's gift to us through our attitude of complaining and dissatisfaction. When Jesus offers himself to us we spend our time debating what we think of him! Let us learn to talk to God more than we talk about him; to come before the mystery with a sense of awe.

Jesus says, 'No one can come to me unless drawn by the Father.' The word which Jesus uses for 'drawn' is the translation of the Hebrew in Jeremiah 31:3 (the Authorised Version has 'With loving kindness I have drawn thee'). The word implies the tugging of God but it also suggests some resistance. The same word is used for tugging a heavy net ashore (John 21:6, 11). God tugs at us in love but we always have the power to resist him. In verse 45 of today's Gospel, Jesus says how all are taught by God, not only the Jews. All are called but all do not listen; all do not react to the tugging of God.

Jesus then repeats how he is the bread of life. Here is an invitation to come to him. Analysis and debate can easily keep you away. With words we can avoid the Word of God. How great is your resistance to his call and his love? There are none so deaf as those who do not want to hear.

Illustration

There was a brilliant scientist who was keen on analysis. He wanted to get to the basic elements of everything. A meal was set before him and he was hungry. But he wanted to check where this food came from and what was in it. He went into his laboratory and started on a loaf of bread. He did not eat any. He checked what its constituents were. He discovered wholemeal flour, water, yeast, vegetable fat, preservatives, emulsifiers and vinegar. He checked out the preservatives and found calcium propionate and potassium sorbate. By now he was starving but research must go on. The emulsifiers kept him busy for ages. He found mono- and diacetyl tartaric acid, esters of mono- and diglycerides, fatty acids. He was kept very busy but he grew weaker and weaker. He still had to analyse the wholemeal and check out the grains. Sadly he died of starvation whilst looking at the loaf. There was food all around him but he died of analysis.

Jesus Feeds 5000

Aim

To show the care and concern of Jesus.

Readings

2 Kings 4:42-44
Psalm 145:10-16
Ephesians 3:14-21
John 6:1-15

Thought for the day

The feeding of the five thousand reveals a good deal about Jesus and his mission.

First, there is the compassion of Jesus. He saw the hunger of the people who had been with him for a good while. He felt for these people who were physically and spiritually hungry. It would have been easy to say, 'There are too many of them; we cannot hope to feed them.' But Jesus has compassion: his heart goes out to them.

Second, there is the challenge of Jesus. He asks Philip, 'Where can we buy bread?' It must have been quite a daunting question when Philip looked at the crowd. Philip estimated that it would take about six months' wages to raise the money to buy enough bread. Jesus was challenging Philip and the disciples to look at their potential and resources. Though our resources are small, they can be greatly transformed if put in God's hands. Andrew seems to rise to the occasion by saying, 'There is a lad here who has five barley loaves and two fish. But what are they among so many?' We often wonder if our small efforts make a difference; well, here we learn they do.

Third is the command of Jesus: 'Make the people sit down.' The disciples were asked to get the people ready for a meal, and then, after the prayer, to distribute it. Jesus does not work alone; he works through us and with us. Without Jesus, we cannot do any great works. Without us, Jesus will not work; he wants us willingly to share with him.

Next is the concern of Jesus. Jesus says, 'Gather up the fragments left over, so that nothing may be lost.' Who would have thought that Jesus, who could feed five thousand with five loaves, would be bothered about crumbs and scraps? Jesus does not want waste: he is concerned how we use the things around us and how we deal with the world. It is good to know Jesus is concerned for the leftovers and that which is lost: they are precious in his sight.

Lastly, notice the caution of Jesus. The people were excited. Some saw the feeding as a 'sign', saying, 'This is indeed the prophet who is to come into the world.' They wanted to take him by force to make him king. Jesus did not come for this kind of kingship or to be a puppet of the people. The people were after Jesus for what they could get out of him. Jesus once again withdrew to the mountain by himself. Yet even in doing this there are hints that Jesus is like Moses who went up on Mount Sinai.

Illustration

There is a story about a boy walking along a beach. All along the shore there were thousands of starfish washed up. You could hardly walk on the sand for them. The boy was putting a few in his bucket and taking them back to the sea. A man came along and said, 'There are thousands of starfish stranded. Why do you bother? You will hardly make an impression. You will only be able to put a few back into the sea.' The boy replied. 'It will matter for these few and it will matter to me.'

Though our effort may be small, it is counted as worthwhile, and who knows what God will do with it?

Holy Communion

Aim

To seek to abide in Jesus and let him abide in us.

Readings

Proverbs 9:1-6
Psalm 34:9-14
1 Corinthians 11:23-25
John 6:51-58

Thought for the day

The Passover and the Eucharist are the setting for this discourse on the 'bread of heaven', and it takes place in the synagogue at Capernaum. At the Passover the Jews are required to eat the unleavened bread and the paschal lamb amongst other things. The Passover remembers the exodus from Egypt, the wandering in the wilderness, including the provision of manna. The reading begins with the words 'I am the living bread that came down from heaven. Whoever eats this bread will live for ever; and the bread that I will give for the life of the world is my flesh.'

Many claims are here. Jesus is still purposely using the words 'I am', which are used as a naming of God. God comes to us in Jesus Christ. It is Jesus who is the living bread. This is a greater offer than Moses', for the children of Israel ate the manna and still died: those who eat this bread from heaven will live for ever. 'The bread that I give for the life of the world is my flesh.' Jesus is not giving us things; he is giving us himself. He offers himself *to* us and offers himself *for* us. He wants us to take of him. We who receive Communion can understand this, and that we abide in him and he in us. The Jews murmured – as ever, analysis prevents the mystery from entering into our lives. The Jews said, 'How can this man give us his flesh to eat?' Surely it is a good question. Do we understand that Jesus was replacing the Passover lamb with his own sacrifice?

Jesus insists, 'Unless you eat the flesh of the Son of Man and drink his blood, you have no life in you.' Unless we take Jesus' life into our life, we will lack the fullness of life. Jesus continues with the theme of mutual indwelling: 'Those who eat my flesh and drink my blood abide in me, and I in them.' This mutual indwelling is the purpose and the joy of every Communion and with it the knowledge that through him we live for ever.

Jesus is not a figure in a book, not even the Bible. He is the living Lord and wants to be one with us. When we abide in him and he in us we have eternal life.

Illustration

There was once a man who bought a beautiful box for his wife. The box had flowers on the top and they would glow in the dark. As it was for her birthday he hid it away in a drawer and left it there for a few weeks. On her birthday it was given to her all wrapped in a lovely parcel. She was delighted and could hardly wait until the evening. When it got dark she looked at the box but it did not shine; it had not changed at all. They both waited until it got really dark but the box never did shine. They felt a little cheated because the box was bought to shine. Then a little note fell from the packaging. It said, 'If you want me to shine all night, you need put me in the sun all day.' The box would only glow if it was left out in the daylight. They left it out all the next day and, true to the words, all night it glowed with a splendid light.

If we are to glow with eternal life, we need to be placed in the presence of the Son of God to let him abide in us and for us to know we abide in him.

GOOD PEOPLE
Saints

Aim
To rejoice in God's saints.

Readings
Wisdom 3:1-9 or Isaiah 25:6-9
Psalm 24:1-6
Hebrews 11:1-2, 39-40; 12:1-2
Matthew 5:1-10

Thought for the day
When a child was asked what is a saint, she replied, 'Someone who lets light in.' She was probably thinking of a stained-glass window. But in a sense she was absolutely right. Saints are like bright lights in a dark world. Through them the light of the Gospel and the glory of the presence of God is revealed. As we look at the lives of the saints we get glimpses of how life ought to be. The saints challenge us in our way of living: they invite us to risk and adventure. The saints challenge our way of looking at the world, our attitude to life and our priorities. Through them we get a glimpse of how we can live to the full and serve God. The saints are not people who diminish their lives but who show us the glorious freedom of the children of God. The saints live their lives to the full to the glory of God. They challenge us to do the same now: to live for God now and to reveal his glory now.

If we make our heroes from the world of sport and the film industry or the fictional characters of the soaps, we may find we are not getting good examples of how to live. To be a good footballer does not guarantee the wisdom to lead a good life. We need men and women of deep and courageous faith to be our guides. We need to know how the saints have lived. We need also to know that there are many people now who are saints revealing God to the world.

Because God wants us to live our lives to the full we often see God choosing people who were far from perfect but had a zest for living. St Francis was called from being a carefree partygoer to show how we can enjoy living for God. Augustine of Hippo was called from living a passionate life with a mistress and a son born out of marriage to show us how to use our passion for God. To be a saint means to have a great appetite for living life to the full.

The saints reveal the love and glory of the Trinity. They share a common union with Father, Son and Holy Spirit and in so doing are part of the Communion of Saints. We are called to be part of that communion. The saints we remember today are not just the great and well-known but those who have no memorials but who lived their lives revealing God's glory and their love for their fellow beings. We rejoice that the souls of the righteous are in the hands of God.

Illustration

The Lantern Saints were a group of early Methodists who lived on the North Yorkshire Moors. They had a meeting place on one of the highest points of the moor at Trough House at the head of Fryup Dale. And people came from outlying farms and hamlets, from the dales of Westerdale, Danby Dale, Farndale, Glaisdale, Rosedale and Great and Little Fryup. It made Trough House look like the centre of a web that spread out into each moorland valley. Often in the winter they struggled up to the moorland height and met in a shuttered room. As each family entered they would light their lantern (a good symbol of receiving the light of the Gospel and the Light of Christ). Once the service was over they would set off in every direction. You could see the light they had received and carried with them travelling to each dale, to farms and homes. From that light they would see in the dark and light other lights. This light was a symbol of how they sought to live by the Light of Christ. These ordinary folk were rightly known locally as the 'Lantern Saints'.

Service and Suffering

Aim

To show that Jesus calls us to serve each other rather than to lord it over people.

Readings

Proverbs 31:10-31
Psalm 1
James 2:14-17; 3:13-18
Mark 9:30-37

Thought for the day

Today's Gospel splits into three parts. In the first part (9:30), Mark shows Jesus seeking to keep his whereabouts a secret. The reasons are twofold. It was a time for teaching his disciples and getting them to understand his purpose and message. It was also necessary to avoid conflict before the disciples had time to understand. This was a precious and important time for Jesus.

In the second part Jesus is predicting his death and resurrection. He is seeking to warn his disciples of what lies ahead, the dangers and the suffering, his death and resurrection. This is important for the disciples to grasp and it is repeated three times (9:31, 8:31 and 10:32-34). We are told that the disciples did not understand what Jesus was saying and were afraid to ask him. No doubt this is part of the reason for the repetition. The disciples found it hard to grasp that God's Anointed One, the Messiah, could be rejected and killed by his own people. To understand the idea of a suffering Messiah was beyond their comprehension. There are still some Christians today who suggest that if only we had more faith we would escape suffering. That is not the way of this world.

The third part is the turning towards Capernaum and back towards Jerusalem and danger. The disciples still think in worldly terms of power – hence their rejection of any idea of the cross or a suffering Christ. They still expect a display of might and when they will share in ruling. When they were on the way back to Capernaum they argued with one another who was the greatest (9:34). In the ancient world, social position was highly ordered; people were expected to stay in 'their place'. The disciples wanted to know their place in the kingdom so that they could get the greatest gain from it. The phrase 'on the way' (33) is the same word as used in Mark 4:14 to describe the seed that got no entry because of Satan taking away any chance of growth. This must have been a very sad time for Jesus. He is willingly going to Jerusalem to offer his life for others and his disciples are arguing among themselves about position and power. Perhaps Judas believed that by betraying Jesus he would make Jesus use force against his enemies.

In 9:35 Jesus assumes the teaching position of a rabbi by sitting down and calling his disciples to him. What Jesus says turns their striving for position upside down – we do well to heed it. Standing, security, satisfaction are not gained by power struggles or beating the Joneses, but by serving. Not from getting and gaining but from giving and grace. The followers of Jesus are called to serve and to give their lives for others as he did.

Jesus illustrates what he means by picking up a little child and taking it in his arms and saying, 'Whoever welcomes one such child in my name welcomes me, and whoever welcomes me, welcomes not me but the one who sent me.' Children had no rights and could make no demands; they had the lowest place in the social order – of course, love made nonsense of such a statement. Being a follower of Jesus means to be willing to give of yourself and to serve. It is not being servile but choosing to give your life to others and for others. By this welcoming of children, or the least, we welcome into our lives not only Jesus the risen Lord but also God. Jesus will emphasise his own desire to serve when James and John are still seeking positions of power. Then he said, 'The Son of Man came not to be served but to serve, and to give his life as a ransom for many' (Mark 10:45).

Illustration

There is a story about a fourth wise man who wanted to come and see the Christ. He started off well. He dressed in his best clothes, rode a fine horse and brought a present of precious stones. On his journey he met a group of poor people who were hungry, so he gave away half of his jewels for them to trade for food. Then he met a family who were taken into slavery because of a debt. He used the rest of his precious jewels to buy their freedom. Further on he found a merchant in deep distress. His horse had died on him and he would not get his goods to be sold on time. The generous wise man gave him his horse and all its trappings. Now he had to walk on foot and the going was slow.

He was old and very weary. He wondered if he would ever see the Christ. The way was very muddy and he met a young family trying to get their cart out of the mud. The wise man helped them but ended up very dirty. He now wondered if he should give up and go home. In a dream he was told, 'The Christ you seek is now only a little distance away. He will welcome you because he knows you. You have met him many times on your journey in the poor and the needy. You soiled your clothes in caring for him. Tomorrow you will meet him and he will welcome you.'

And so it was.

Good Inside and Out

Aim

To understand what it means to be good on the inside as well as the outside.

Readings

Deuteronomy 4:1-2, 6-9
Psalm 15
James 1:17-27 or Galatians 5:22-25
Mark 7:1-8, 14-15, 21-23

Thought for the day

It is hard to believe that the Pharisees would travel all the way from Jerusalem to Galilee to tell Jesus that he and his disciples had dirty hands. This meeting is about confrontation and it shows how Jesus was challenging the attitudes of the established church.

The Pharisees say that Jesus and his disciples are unclean. They have not washed properly before eating bread. Very often Jesus did things that made him unclean in the eyes of the Pharisees. He touched a leper; he touched a bier on which there was a dead man. A woman who was suffering from a haemorrhage touched him. Jesus was declared unclean by each of these acts, and anyone who was in contact with him became unclean also.

The Jewish rituals of washing were mainly good common sense. They were safeguards against infection and harmful contacts. In the same way, we know we ought to wash after doing a dirty job or going to the toilet. But with the tradition becoming fixed there was a danger that someone felt they could do something they ought not to and then just wash their hands and be clean. Within the Christian Church some people have misused the practice of confession. We cannot truly seek forgiveness of a sin if we intend to go on committing it. We cannot come to church on a Sunday for absolution if we intend to do the same things again.

Jesus replied that it was no use going through outward rituals if the inside is not cleansed. A show of being clean is just pretence. Jesus calls the Pharisees hypocrites. Originally a hypocrite was a play actor; it meant one who pretends or gives a set reply. It came to mean a person whose life was an act without depth or sincerity. Anyone who goes through the religious acts or rituals without a relationship to God is a hypocrite. Cleanliness does not depend on whether you have washed or eaten; it depends on your inner attitude, on your thoughts and your heart. It is no use being present at worship if we do not give ourselves to our God. This is why the Psalmist prayed, 'Make me a clean heart, O God, and renew a right Spirit within me.' We must be sure our human traditions do not come between God and us. Maybe this would make Christians take a careful look at how we keep Christmas for instance.

Jesus lists among the things that defile a person evil intentions or designs. Every outward act of sin comes from an inward choice. We need to keep watch on our thoughts and our decisions. Very often our departure from goodness and from God begins with the attitudes and choices that we make. If we fail to give God the central place in our thinking, we will soon push him to the edges of our life.

Another word Jesus uses about defilement is translated as 'fornications'. It is from the Greek word 'porneiai' and means every kind of sexual vice. We must include all pornography and wrong attitudes towards sex. Anything that degrades others or ourselves makes us unclean. We need keep a close watch on our attitudes and what we expose our minds to.

Illustration

A devout Muslim carries his prayer mat around with him and prays a fixed number of times each day. At the fixed times he will unroll his mat and turn to God. This is a wonderful way of keeping in contact with his Creator.

There was a certain Muslim who had great anger in his heart. He was in hot pursuit of a man whom he wanted to kill. He had a dagger and was intent on murder. Suddenly the call to prayer rang out from the mosque. The man stopped for a moment, rushed his prayers, then continued on his murderous chase. The prayer was part of his daily ritual but he did not let it touch his heart. This man could be seen to be a hypocrite.

ADVENT
Waiting for God

Aim
To make people more aware that Christ comes to them today.

Readings
Isaiah 64:1-9
Psalm 80:1-7,17-19
1 Corinthians 1:3-9
Mark 13:24-37 or Luke 12:35-40

Thought for the day
Happy New Year! This is the first Sunday in the Church Year. We celebrate the Church's New Year by lighting a candle. It is called an Advent candle. Advent is about the coming of God into the world.

Isaiah sees God's coming as something that is frightening, because we have not been looking for our God; in fact, we have been ignoring him. God has been coming to us and we have not let him into our lives. But because God has made us and loves us, he will have mercy upon us. We may annoy our parents, we may ignore them, but they still continue to love us and care for us. We are not alone in the world; if we seek God he comes to us.

Psalm 80 has the refrain 'Show us the light of your countenance and we shall be saved.' We ask the hide-and-seek God to reveal himself to us. Let us learn to look for God in our everyday life.

God has shown himself to us in the face of Jesus Christ. In Jesus we have a new hope, for God's grace – that is the free gift of himself – has been given to us in Christ Jesus. This is a gift to each of us. Will we unwrap this gift and make it ours, that he may enrich us?

The Gospels tell us not to put off, or be put off, for the Son of Man comes. The times may be full of trouble and distress, yet he still comes to us. We should look for signs of his coming and of his presence in our lives.

We have been left in charge of this world, each with our own responsibility, each with our own work. We are accountable to God. He comes to see how we are dealing with his world. We need to keep alert, that we may be aware of his coming: to be awake and not go around with our eyes closed.

Illustration

It was near Christmas and in the Advent season, and Peter waited for God to come. He prayed every day, 'God, show me your face and I shall be saved.' Peter had tried to live a good life; he was now old and looked forward to the coming of God. He continued to work in his paper shop, where he had worked most of his life. Here he heard all sorts of conversations and met many people. A single mum was telling a friend how she did not have enough money to buy presents for her child. When everyone else had gone, Peter said to her, 'I heard what you said. I have a few toys on the shelves; they are not selling very well, go and pick anything you would like.' She could hardly believe it for there were some wonderful things on the shelves. As she went away with her arms full, Peter was delighted. His reward was her smile.

Later that day, he caught a young lad stealing a magazine from the shelves. He was on the way out with the magazine up his jumper when Peter stopped him. He could have called the police or told the boy's parents. He saw the boy was poor and afraid, and he felt sorry for him. 'If you want a magazine, and have no money, talk with me,' he said. 'Magazines are soon out of date; I can always find one to give you. You must not just help yourself. Take the magazine for free and ask me another time.' The boy's face changed from a look of fear to a beaming smile. He thanked Peter and ran from the shop.

An old man came into the shop and was saying how lonely he was since his wife died. This would be his first Christmas on his own – he was not looking forward to it. Peter said, 'We were expecting a friend to come for Christmas, and he has said he cannot make it. We have prepared for his coming. Would you come to us instead? We would love to share Christmas with you.' The old man's face lit up in a beautiful smile and he said, 'You have made me feel so wanted, and I would love to come.'

That night Peter prayed his Advent prayer, 'Show me your face and I shall be saved.' In a dream God spoke to him and said, 'Peter, today I came to you, and three times you made me smile. Grace and peace be upon you.'

(Apologies to Tolstoy!)

Prepared?

Aim

To show we need to prepare for the coming of our Lord.

Readings

Isaiah 40:1-11
Psalm 85:1-2, 8-13
2 Peter 3:8-15a
Mark 1:1-8

Thought for the day

Isaiah is sure that our God is coming to us and that we need to prepare. He tells us of the messenger that will go before his coming to see all is ready. In the olden days, when travel was difficult and dangerous, if a king was on a journey someone was sent ahead to see if the road was fit for a king. The aim was to remove obstacles in the road, to fill in holes and to level off bumps: rough places were made smooth. Then they had to make sure the king would get a good reception, that accommodation was prepared, making sure there was room for the king and he would be welcome. Once everything was ready the king would come in all his glory.

Today's psalm asks, 'Show us your steadfast love, O Lord, and grant us your salvation . . . that his glory may dwell in our land.'

St Peter is also sure that the Lord will come, and asks what sort of person you will be when he comes. Will you be a holy and a godly person? Do not put things off, for you do not know when the Lord will come. Strive to be found at peace.

St Mark is sure that Jesus is the Promised One and that John the Baptist is the messenger to prepare his way. John says to the people, 'Turn around; you are going the wrong way. You will not be ready for God if you go on like this. Repent and be cleansed. Say sorry for the wrong you have done and turn to God.'

Illustration

The Sunday before the beginning of Advent used to be called 'Stir up Sunday' for two reasons. The prayer for the Sunday begins, 'Stir up, O Lord, the wills of your faithful people'; a wonderful prayer that wants us to 'bring forth the fruits of good works'. It is by what we do that we will be known, so it is important that our works are good, important that we do something.

Traditionally 'Stir up Sunday' was also the time when the Christmas cake was made. Mother would get all the ingredients – the flour, the fruit, the eggs – and mix them together. Everyone in the house had a stir of the cake before it went into the oven. All this was part of the preparations before Christmas.

We now often spend weeks preparing for this one day. How much time do we spend preparing for the coming of God to us?

If someone is coming to stay, we will make sure there is room for them, that we have time for them, that we will give them some attention. Our God comes and seeks room in our lives; he wants us to be aware of him, for us to give him some of our time and attention.

Are you prepared for this?

The Messiah

Aim

To encourage people to see that Jesus comes in acts of kindness and righteousness.

Readings

Isaiah 61:1-4, 8-11
Psalm 126 or the Magnificat (Luke 1:46-55)
1 Thessalonians 5:16-24
John 1:6-8, 19-28

Thought for the day

Jesus chose to speak on this passage from Isaiah and relate it to his ministry. He was the 'anointed one', the Messiah. In his baptism the Spirit of the Lord was seen to descend upon him.

The Lord wants us to share in his mission. We are asked to bring the Good News to the poor – surely everyone who has not heard and received the Good News is poor! We are called to bind up the broken-hearted, to proclaim liberty for captives, and to comfort all who mourn. We must remember the Lord loves justice and hates wrongdoing.

In both the psalm and the Magnificat there is a feeling of the new order beginning, when God's people are freed to do righteous acts.

The writer to the Thessalonians asks us to 'hold fast to that which is good: abstain from every evil'.

Illustration

Once upon a time there was a man who went out to sea in a little boat. It was a lovely day and he was enjoying himself. Then the mist suddenly came down. Now he did not know which direction he was going in. He rowed around until he was very tired, then he let himself drift. He did not know that he was drifting towards the rocks. Suddenly he heard a crunch and a scraping. His boat was torn on the rocks and it began to sink. Fortunately he managed to escape on to the rocks. He was now very cold and hungry and he prayed to God to come and rescue him.

Soon a motorboat came by and invited him aboard – but he refused, saying, 'I have help coming.' A little later a fishing boat saw him and tried to persuade him to come off the rock but again he said, 'There is no need to worry I have help on the way.'

That night the man died alone in the cold. He went to heaven and complained to God that he had not come to help. God said, 'I came in a motorboat and you refused my help. I came again in a fishing boat and you still refused my help. You are here today because you did not recognise my help when it came – yet still you are loved.'

Welcome?

Aim

To show God's kingdom comes when his will is done.

Readings

2 Samuel 7:1-11, 16
Magnificat (Luke 1:46-55) or Psalm 89:1-4, 19-26
Romans 16:25-27
Luke 1:26-38 or Luke 2:1-7

Thought for the day

David is aware that he lives in a good house and that God's dwelling is only a tent. He wants to build a splendid house for God. It is a wonderful idea but the danger is that we may feel we can only find God in his house. At least with a tent God was travelling with the Israelites: when they moved, God moved with them. God also says to David, 'I have been with you wherever you went.'

God promises David that he will make him a house and a kingdom that will last for ever. God will be ever-present within it.

The love that God showed to David is celebrated in Psalm 89. In the same way Mary praises God for the great things he has done and shall do for ever.

St Paul tells us that this same God is able to strengthen us through Jesus Christ, to whom all glory belongs.

God will not force himself upon us. If we lock him out, he will not break down the doors. If we ignore him, he will still care for us and love us. If we do not obey him, his kingdom cannot come in us. But once we say, 'Here am I; let it be to me according to your word', then the kingdom is come in us. Notice how God and the angel wait upon Mary's response. Without Mary, or someone like her, the Son of God cannot come into the world. When Mary says 'Yes' a new age begins. Let us learn to pray, 'Your kingdom come in us. Your will be done in us.'

When we obey the king, his kingdom comes in us.

Illustration

Are you ready for Christmas? Have you sent all your cards? Bought presents? Got the food ready? What will you do on Christmas Day? Will you make room for Jesus: make sure Christ is in Christ-mas?

It was Jessie's birthday and she looked forward to it. She lived in an old people's home and had friends around her – but she was invited to her daughter's for her birthday. She would be with the family, including the three children. They made sure there was a nice room ready for her and the house was warm. Her daughter had bought the food she liked. All was ready.

On the first night her daughter had an evening class, the children were out with friends, and her son-in-law decided to go to the pub. On her birthday the children had other things to do and so would be out all day – football, swimming and netball are important. Jessie's son-in-law spent the day in the garage tinkering with his car, and her daughter decided to do some last-minute shopping on her own. Again Jessie was left alone. They had a meal together in the evening, then the children went on the computer and the others watched television. Jessie was glad to go back to the home where people had time to talk to her and give their attention to her.

Will we make time for Jesus on his birthday, or will we be too busy doing other things?

CHRISTMAS
Shepherds and Angels

Aim

To show that the people involved in the birth of Jesus were ordinary people involved in an extraordinary event.

Readings

Isaiah 61:10–62:3
Psalm 148
Galatians 4:4-7
Luke 2:8-21

Thought for the day

Isaiah invites us to rejoice in the Lord and in his salvation. Likewise the psalm asks us to praise the name of the Lord; to join in with all creation and give him praise. This should be our aim throughout our worship.

God's promised time has come and his Son is born of the Blessed Virgin Mary. Like the shepherds, we are invited to glorify and praise God.

The shepherds were very ordinary men who worked on the hillsides tending sheep. By the nature of their job they rarely went to church – but that did not prevent God from knowing them and them from knowing God. They saw the angels, not because they were good but because God is good and comes to ordinary people in ordinary places. Shepherds on a hillside, Mary and Joseph travelling on a road, stars in the sky and a stable for a birth are all ordinary and familiar. We know these things and we can experience them, but it is only half the picture.

Show a negative and explain what it is. A negative is not a black and white photograph or a photograph without colour. If you look at a negative it is sometimes hard to see what the picture is, but it has the potential of making a picture. The negative is important but it is only half the picture. A print is necessary for us to see and understand the whole picture.

We all know about the shepherds and sheep but the other part of the picture makes the whole picture – angels and God are to be discovered. Our world is full of mystery, wonder and a presence. Our minds cannot wholly grasp the mystery but our hearts can. Let us spend some time today thinking upon God and his love.

There are not two separate worlds: heaven and earth are one. God is with us. It is our own lack of vision that prevents us from seeing this.

Illustration

Sally was naughty at school. She did not pay attention to what was written on the board, nor was she all that keen on being out in the country because she was not really interested in the flowers or the birds. A beautiful scene did not move her with joy. Starry nights did not fill her with awe. Then it was discovered that Sally was very short-sighted and needed glasses. She had not been able to see what was around her, so her world and her life were restricted by her vision. Once she had glasses the world became a place full of wonder and beauty. She loved going out into the country to enjoy the scenery, to watch the birds and see the flowers. Once Sally saw more clearly, her whole world changed.

EPIPHANY
Christ for all Peoples

Aim

To show how the Christ was revealed to all nations.

Readings

Isaiah 60:1-6
Psalm 72:8-15
Ephesians 3:1-12
Matthew 2:1-12

Thought for the day

Many of the Jews believed that the Christ would only be for their own nation: they were the chosen people and no other. Yet throughout the Scriptures there are suggestions that the Christ was for all peoples. Today's readings are chosen to show this. Isaiah asks the Jews to arise and shine because their light has come and the glory of the Lord is risen upon them. Isaiah goes on to say that nations and kings will come to that light. He even says they will bring gifts of gold and frankincense (Isaiah 60:1, 3, 6). Psalm 72 also declares, 'All kings shall bow before him and all nations do him service'.

St Paul declares how he was given a revelation to perceive that the Gentiles had become sharers in the promise of Christ through the Gospel (Ephesians 3:4). So, we, who are among the Gentiles, have access to God in boldness and confidence through Christ.

The fulfilment of the prophecy is seen in the coming of the wise men, who are Gentiles, to the Christ – they are the first of the rest of the world.

Illustration

The wise men were not all that wise because they went to the wrong place and the wrong person. They went to the capital, Jerusalem, and to King Herod. Fancy asking him, 'Where is he who is to be born king of the Jews?' Herod hadn't a clue but he knew who would know about the Messiah, about the Christ. He asked the chief priests and scribes. They told him, 'In Bethlehem in the land of Judah.' Lucky for the wise men it was only about seven miles away. Herod sent them off and told them to search diligently for the child and to tell him when they had found him. Fortunately, the wise men did not trust Herod or his interest in the Christ child.

We assume there were three because we are told of three gifts. We know that they were rich, foreign and wise, but we do not know that they were kings. The shepherds were ordinary Jews smelling of sheep and probably not able to read or write. These men were different indeed, almost in total contrast. It helps us to see God calls all peoples to come to him – rich and poor, the known and the stranger, simple and wise; all are invited to come to God.

JESUS
Baptism

Aim
To encourage people to think about baptism and the Holy Trinity.

Readings
Genesis 1:1-5
Psalm 51:1-12
Acts 19:1-7
Mark 1:4-11

Thought for the day
At the beginning of creation we hear of the Creator, the word of God and the wind (Spirit) of God.

St Paul asked the disciples at Ephesus if they had received the Holy Spirit. They replied they were baptised by John the Baptist and had not heard of the Holy Spirit. Water baptism and repentance was not enough; they needed to be baptised in the name of the Lord Jesus and to receive the gift of the Holy Spirit.

Today many people are baptised in water but they are hardly aware that they are immersed in the presence of Father, Son and Holy Spirit. Such people are like the people Paul met at Ephesus. We need to see that our baptism in water is an outward and visible sign of our immersion in the presence of Father, Son and Holy Spirit. Each day we should rejoice that we are in the presence and power of Father, Son and Holy Spirit.

Jesus came to John to be baptised. He did not need to come to repent; he came to commit himself to the next stage of his life and mission. Jesus shared in our humanity and his baptism was part of his identification with us. Furthermore, it was a sign of approval and his anointing; he was now equipped for the task for which he came. The Spirit comes upon him and the voice of the Father is heard. Here we have a brief glimpse of the Holy Trinity. There is also a feeling that it is like the beginning of creation – a new world is about to begin. In the same way, the dove comes as it came to Noah after the flood destroyed the old world. Something new is about to happen.

Illustration

Have a nice mug, which is empty. Get people to admire it, tell them how beautiful it is – but it is useless unless it has something in it – it is no use empty! Only when it has something in it does it fulfil its purpose. People and their minds are the same: we are no use if we are empty.

Borrow a jacket or a fleece, lay it before you and admire it. How good it is for keeping out the cold. Now command it to raise an arm or to sit up straight. When it fails to act, say you know a secret way of getting it to do things. Now get the owner to put it on and raise an arm. The jacket is of no use unless it is occupied.

Nature abhors a vacuum – something will always fill an empty space. Let us be filled and immersed in Father, Son and Holy Spirit.

At a Wedding

Aim

To show that miracles are mysteries and signs of the kingdom.

Readings

Genesis 14:17-20
Psalm 133
Revelation 19:6-10
John 2:1-11

Thought for the day

All of today's readings are full of mystery. There is King Melchizedek who meets Abram and brings him bread and wine; Revelation invites us to the marriage supper of the Lamb.

We will concentrate on the Gospel and, according to St John, the first miracle of Jesus.

Miracles are wonderful events that we cannot fully explain – if we could, they would not be miracles. We are to see each miracle as a sign of the kingdom of heaven and the kingship of Christ.

The first miracle is a joyful occasion for it is a wedding. For the people who lived in Cana, weddings were usually held on a Wednesday evening. The couple would wear wedding robes and crowns on their heads. They would be treated like a king and a queen. This might be the greatest celebration of their life. They would be led home by torchbearers filling the street with light. A canopy would be carried over their heads, just like royalty. They would not go away for a honeymoon but would have 'open house' and a party, which would last for a week! That would take a lot of planning. There would be lots of guests and they would all wash their hands and their feet when they came to the house. There were large water jars outside for this purpose.

Jesus, his mother and disciples were at the party. It is thought that the bride or groom might have been a relative of Jesus. Cana was near Nazareth where Jesus lived.

There was singing and dancing and all were enjoying themselves. Suddenly Mary said to Jesus, 'They have no wine.' The party was not meant to end but soon it would be over. The wine had run out. The bride and groom would be embarrassed for they had run out of resources.

Jesus looked at the six big water jars that had been used for washing. Each jar held between 20 and 30 gallons. Jesus said to the servants, 'Fill the water pots.' They filled them right to the top. 'Now,' said Jesus, 'take some to the steward who is in charge.' They obeyed Jesus again. When the steward tasted the water it had become wine. He called the bridegroom and said, 'Everyone serves good wine first. But you have kept the best until now.' He did not know of the miracle; only the servants knew. You can imagine the surprise of the groom. The party could go on and people could enjoy themselves.

Illustration

Have you ever heard of Dracula? Dracula is supposed to come when you are asleep and drain away your life. When you wake up in the morning you are at least half dead. It is not a true story but sometimes we can wake exhausted; we can feel we have no energy. Human resources do run out. Our batteries need recharging; we need to be refreshed and renewed.

When we feel we have reached the bottom of the barrel we need outside help. There are times when we are unable to help ourselves but Jesus is able to help us. In John 10:10, Jesus says, 'I came that they may have life, and have it abundantly.' You can trace this giving of abundant life, and how Jesus meets various needs and losses of well-being, in John's Gospel:

Need more wine – 2:1-11
Loss of well-being – 4:46-54
Lack strength – 5:2-9
Lack energy (food) – 6:1-14
Lack of security and safety – 6:16-21
Lack of vision and light – 9:1-7
Loss of life – 11:1-44

Jesus meets our drained resources with his generosity and power.

Sent with God's Love

Aim

To encourage people to wonder at the mystery of God's love in Jesus Christ.

Readings

Ecclesiasticus 24:1-12 and Wisdom 10:15-21
Ephesians 1:3-14
John 1: 10-18

Thought for the day

All the readings are about God caring for his chosen people and coming to them as their Redeemer. They tell of the Word of God, or the Wisdom of God, taking flesh and dwelling among us. All of today's readings can be seen as songs of praise.

The reading from Ephesians is amazing in that it is all one sentence in the Greek. Here St Paul is pouring out his praise to God for caring for us and calling us. Notice how it starts, like many Jewish prayers of praise, saying, 'Blessed be God.'

It starts in a surprising way by telling us how God chose us before the world began. No, we did not choose God; he chose us (see John 15:16). He wants us to be part of his team! He wants us to be holy – that is, to belong to him – and he wants us to be blameless – without sin – before him in love (Ephesians 1, verses 3-4).

Out of his goodness and grace – for we do not deserve it – God wants us to be part of his family and to enjoy all the privileges of belonging with him as our Father, through Jesus Christ (verses 5-6).

In Jesus we have redemption; he has bought our freedom through his own death. He has ransomed us from death. Through him our sins are forgiven – not because we deserve this but through the riches of his grace that he has lavished upon us (verses 7-8).

God has made known to us the mystery of his will, to gather up all things in Christ. Divisions disappear and all are one in him, not absorbed but fulfilled in him (verses 9-10).

In Christ, because we are made part of God's family, we obtain an inheritance. In him we have heard the word, the Good News of salvation, and as an assurance of this we have received the Holy

Spirit. As God's people let us live to praise his glory.

Wow! What a lot Paul packs into a sentence!

You could say John summarises this and says, 'And the Word became flesh and lived among us, and we have seen his glory, the glory as of a Father's only Son, full of grace and truth' (John 1:14).

Illustration

I get tired of letters through the door that say you have been especially chosen – I know that everyone is getting such a letter. Then it tells me I have won £10,000 – whoopee! But the small print says, 'if my number comes up', and the real chances of that are more than a million to one.

God is not like that. God's offer is not gifts (though he does offer us them); he offers himself to us in Jesus Christ our Lord. We do not deserve this; we cannot win it. God has chosen to give himself to us. All we have to do is accept his presence and his love.

The Good Shepherd

Aim

To show how much the Good Shepherd cares for us and will do for us.

Readings

Ezekiel 34:11-15
Psalm 23
1 John 3:16-24
John 10:11-18

Thought for the day

In most jobs there are those who work because they love what they are doing and those who only do it for the money. The people who only work for money rarely get as much pleasure out of their work. Those who are in it just for the money rarely choose dangerous work or work that demands some personal sacrifice.

In the time of Jesus, being a shepherd was recognised as a dangerous occupation. When he was a shepherd, David had to battle with a lion and a bear (1 Samuel 17:34-36). Isaiah tells of a group of shepherds coming together to chase a lion (Isaiah 31:4). Added to the risk from wild animals was the risk from thieves and robbers. A shepherd was called to risk his life for the sheep.

The false shepherd, when he saw trouble coming, would run away. He did not really care for the sheep; he certainly would not risk his life for them. It is not sensible to die for a few sheep. They were not worth it.

The good shepherd loved his sheep. He knew them by name and they knew him. Because of his love he would risk his life for the sheep; he would lay down his life for them. The false shepherd would say that was stupid. Is not a human worth more than the sheep? You will not be able to answer that question unless you understand about love.

Jesus died on the cross for us before we ever turned to him or loved him. You could argue it was not worth the Son of God suffering for us. He did it because of his love for us. Not even because we loved him but because he loved us. He could have avoided the crucifixion; he could have called down help from heaven. Then he would not have died for us and we would not have been saved from death. Out of love and obedience to the will of the Father, Jesus gave himself willingly for us and rose again for us.

Jesus reminds the Pharisees that his love was not exclusive: 'There are other sheep not of this fold.' Because of the outreach and love of Jesus, the Church can never be exclusive. We need to reach out and share in his rescuing and redeeming work.

Illustration

There was a group of shepherds who often talked about caring for their sheep. Yet, when trouble came, some did not want to bother; others said the sheep were not worth the risk; one or two took the money and left. One could be heard saying, 'You cannot believe a lamb is worth the life of a shepherd.' The reply from a hired man was, 'Of course it is not.'

Listening to all this was the good shepherd. It made him sad to think that the sheep were not truly loved. He loved his sheep dearly and would do anything to save them. Suddenly an old man came to him and said, 'I have been looking at your flock and you have a ewe lamb missing. She has wandered off and is in danger of death.' The shepherd left the comfort of home and the safety of his surroundings and began the search. Some were sure he should not have bothered. There were plenty of other sheep; why bother with a wayward one? The shepherd's life was more precious than the lamb's. The shepherd was soon travelling dark valleys. More than once he was at risk himself. Briars tore at his hands and his feet. There was a gaping hole in his side. Thorns had pierced his head. He was calling the lamb by name. At last there was a weak response. It was down a steep slope and in danger of falling further. The shepherd did not fear but descended into the depths. The darkness was trying to hold on to the lamb. The shepherd reached into the thorn bushes and became entangled; he was caught alongside the lamb. Even now he reached out to comfort it. There he lay, life ebbing out of him. He was trapped for more than 48 hours. But on the third day he broke free and rising up brought the lamb with him. He carried it all the way home. When they saw him they rejoiced. 'Just see how much he loves his flock and what he was willing to suffer for one little ewe lamb.'

The Transfiguration

Aim

To show that Jesus is the Son of God and fulfils the longings of the law and the prophets.

Readings

Exodus 24:12-18
Psalm 50:1-6
2 Corinthians 4:3-6, 16-18
Mark 9:2-9

Thought for the day

A week before the events in today's Gospel the disciples were at Caesarea Philippi. It was there that Peter had confessed Jesus as the 'Christ' and there that Jesus told them of the suffering ahead. Perhaps there was a need for some of the disciples at least to see some brightness behind the dark clouds that threatened.

Jesus took Peter, James and John up a mountainside for them to be alone. Tradition says this was Mount Tabor but this is a good way from Caesarea Philippi and it has a fortress on the top. It is more likely to have been Mount Hermon. Maybe they even went up to the snow line.

What happened on the mountain was an experience the disciples could not put into words. They became aware of the radiance of Jesus and of the presence of Moses and Elijah. In Jesus they were aware that all that Moses and Elijah had hoped for was fulfilled. Like Moses, Jesus would bring his people to the freedom of the Promised Land. He would give them a new way of life and free them from slavery. Elijah was said to be the greatest of the prophets. Now, in Jesus, all the hopes of the prophets were to be fulfilled. In the Christ is the second Moses and the second Elijah whom the people of God longed for. Such a vision would carry the disciples a long way, but there was more: the cloud that overshadowed them was hiding the presence of the Father. God was there in his fullness but for their sake his glory had to be hidden. As God had appeared to Moses in the cloud, now he was present on this mountain. Then there was the voice from the cloud saying, 'This is my Son, the Beloved, listen to him!'

Then the vision faded and they descended the mountain and made their way to Jerusalem. But they had been there; they had a glimpse of the glory of God as revealed in Jesus Christ.

We are offered a glimpse of this glory as we move towards Lent and beyond that to the events of Holy Week. We are also asked to 'Listen to him!' Listening also means obeying.

Listen again to the words of St Paul:

For it is the God who said,
'Let light shine out of darkness',
who has shone in our hearts
to give the light of the knowledge of the glory of God
in the face of Jesus Christ.
2 Corinthians 4:6

Even when the vision faded the disciples had their eyes fixed on looking at Jesus. We seek in the days ahead to look at Jesus and to get a glimpse of the glory of God.

Illustration

The day before the civil rights campaigner Martin Luther King was killed by a sniper's bullet he said words of encouragement to a large crowd:

> We've got difficult days ahead. But it does not matter to me now. Because I have been to the mountain top, I won't mind. Like anyone else I would like to live a long life . . . but I am not concerned about that now. I just want to do God's will. And he's allowed me to go up the mountain. And I have looked over and seen the Promised Land. So I am happy tonight, I am not fearing any man. Mine eyes have seen the glory of the coming of the Lord.

Like Martin Luther King, if we are to survive dark days, we need to have a vision of the glory of our God.

More than Possessions

Aim

To show that God wants all of us and not just gifts and prayers.

Readings

Jeremiah 9:23-24
Psalm 119:9-16
1 Timothy 6:17-19
Mark 10:17-31

Thought for the day

It seems some people have everything going for them. Today we hear of a rich man coming to Jesus. St Matthew tells us the man is young (19:20). St Luke tells us he is a ruler (18:18): he is a rich young ruler – obviously God has blessed him. We also learn that he keeps the commandments. Now he comes asking what he should do to gain eternal life. He comes running to Jesus and throws himself at his feet. Surely here is a chance of a useful disciple. There is something startling about this situation when this rich young man of authority throws himself at the feet of a penniless wanderer from Nazareth.

Jesus seems to be hard on this man. Maybe it was the way the question was phrased. First, there is a bit of flattery – 'Good Master' – and then 'what must I do to gain . . .' It would seem this man was in the business of making a profit. He did not come to give of himself but to gain for himself. He already had many blessings but he wanted more. No doubt he was willing to give something for it. But Jesus replies that the man cannot pay the price. God does not want things instead of ourselves; he does not even want prayers or sacrifices unless we can give ourselves to him. Obedience to commandments is good but God wants more: he wants our love.

There is always the danger of being possessed by things. Instead of owning things, they begin to own us and we become possessed by our possessions – or some of us are possessed by the lack of them! We spend much of our lives seeking to gain, to get, to have, and we can be in danger of losing sight of loving and giving of ourselves. Money can be a good reflection of this. Some people's pockets are as hard to touch as their hearts.

Here was a man given a glorious opportunity; the same one that was offered to Matthew when he was at the tax desk: 'Leave it all and follow me.' Jesus invited this man to a great adventure, offered him the way to eternal life. But he went away grieving, and it is possible he would grieve for ever. Why did he grieve? Because 'he had many possessions'. He could not enter into the fullness of life because of the things that were around him. This is surely one of the most tragic stories of the Gospels and a warning to all of us.

Illustration

Imagine a table. I want you to put on it all the things you want to give to God: your time, talents, money; your home, your friends, your loved ones; your job, your plans, your future.

You are going to need a great big table. We raise up the things we want to give to God and say, 'All things come from you, O God, and of your own do we give you.'

But wait, one thing that God wants is still missing. Who knows what it is?

GOD WANTS YOU.

More than any gift, more than gold or silver, God wants you.

God wants you to give yourself to him.

God wants you to give your love.

God wants you more than anything.

St Paul said, 'If I give away all my possessions . . . but do not have love, I gain nothing' (1 Corinthians 13:3).

For or Against?

Aim
To show how Jesus risked safety and security for us.

Readings
Isaiah 5:18-21
Psalm 34:11-22
1 Peter 5:6-11
Mark 3:20-35

Thought for the day
Jesus was very popular with the ordinary people: wherever he went crowds followed him. He went into a house and the crowd that followed was so large that Jesus and his disciples did not even have time to eat. It was not the first time this had happened and his family was worried for him. They loved him and wanted to protect him. They came to where he was because people were saying, 'He has gone out of his mind.'

Jesus had left the security of Nazareth for a life on the road. His work as a carpenter in Nazareth must have provided Jesus with a good way of life. He would have his family around him; there would be love and care. His family thought it was foolish to leave this to become a wandering preacher who did not have time to eat.

Not only did Jesus leave his security behind; he left the safety of a peaceful life. He was running into trouble with the religious leaders. There are some people whom it is better not to upset and Jesus was upsetting them. Very soon, if not already, Jesus' life would be in danger. He would be safer at home in Nazareth.

He wanted to lead people and show them a better way of life. But look at the people he gathered around him – they were neither learned nor great strong characters. He chose fishermen, a traitorous tax collector and a freedom fighter to be part of his team. He risked society laughing at him. Out of love, his family wanted to take him home.

Jesus could not go with them. He would risk his life for us. He would leave safety and security behind and go on the road towards the cross.

As his family loved him, another group was out to condemn him. The Scribes had followed from Jerusalem, not because they believed or loved him but because they wanted to find fault. They could not deny that Jesus healed people: they actually saw it happen. They tried to frighten people off Jesus by saying he was in league with Beelzebul. This was a pagan god and the name means 'lord of the flies'. They suggested that Jesus worked for Satan, the ruler of demons.

Jesus pointed out how wicked it was to say this. Evil would not fight evil (evil fights goodness). To call good evil is wicked and perverts life.

Jesus accepted that life is a struggle between good and evil, and there is no doubt on which side he stood. Jesus regarded healing as a defeat of evil. He wanted people to be whole and healthy. Jesus cared for the whole person – body, mind and spirit – and not just part of them.

He confronted the Scribes. This was a great risk but he was determined to stand against evil. By their attitude, the Scribes separated themselves from Jesus.

Illustration

Jesus risked his own safety and security for us. As Christians, we are often called to share in this risky adventure. The call is often like the call to the man with the withered hand: 'Come forward . . . stretch out' (Mark 3:3, 5).

Very often the Church hides behind set services and conventions. The words and the patterns are fixed so that no one is disturbed. Jesus calls, 'Come forward.' Stand where everyone can see you. Where every fault-finding eye can fall upon you. Where those who reject Jesus can vent themselves upon you. 'Safety first' is not our policy: the Church is not meant to be hidden – 'Come forward' for Jesus. Then 'stretch out', even if you feel your talent has withered. Attempt the impossible for God, trusting in his power. Take risks for God and let him work through you. The call of Jesus to the man with the withered hand is a call to the Church to let him work through us. Come forward . . . stretch out.

Master of Storms

Aim

To learn to turn to Jesus in the storms of life.

Readings

Job 38:1-11
Psalm 107:1-3, 23-32
2 Corinthians 6:1-10
Mark 4:35-41

Thought for the day

Jesus was exhausted. People had been coming day and night. He had hardly had time even to eat. He had been pouring himself out until there was little left and he needed space and refreshment. He got into the boat and was asleep almost straightaway. There he is in the stern sleeping.

Peter scans the sky and does not like the look of it. The wind is rising; the sea is becoming restless. From the heights of Mount Hermon and the hills and valleys around, funnelled through the ravines, winds descend without warning and with great force. Voyagers on the Sea of Galilee often met such storms. The disciples understood that only God could still the storm and bring calm; humans would do best to stay out of it if they could.

Suddenly the storm hits the little boat. There is little the fishermen can do. They cannot escape and their boat is filling with water. Jesus continues to sleep. The boat is in the midst of chaos: the canvas is out of control, the helm won't respond, timber and tackle groan. Like many before them it seems they could be lost at sea. They are fighting for survival and they call upon Jesus, 'Teacher, do you not care that we are perishing?'

Jesus wakes up and rebukes the wind and says to the waves, 'Peace! Be still.' Then the wind ceases and there is a dead calm.

(Read from Psalm 107:28-29.) The words of the Psalm were applied to God only. No wonder the disciples were filled with awe and asked, 'Who is this that even the wind and the sea obey him?' To this there is one answer only: Jesus is God.

Illustration

Do you know the story of Aladdin and his lamp? The lamp had wonderful powers but most people did not recognise it. The lamp standing unused was no better than any other. It could give out a little light but its great power remained untapped. It is no use having a wonderful power if you do not use it. In the same way, it is no use saying you believe in a Saviour if you do not call upon him.

Too often we allow Jesus to sleep in our lives. We struggle on alone and are often overwhelmed because we do not call upon him in the storm. While we allow fear to mount and energies to be overpowered, we fail to call upon the greatest power, which is our Lord.

In the storms of fear and sorrow, when we are feeling overwhelmed, we need to know the presence and the power of our God. We need to know again that God can bring order out of chaos and that Christ can give us his peace. Do not let Jesus sleep in your life; call upon him each day. Take heed these words from Julian of Norwich:

> He said not: 'Thou shalt not be tempest-tossed; thou shalt not be work-weary; thou shalt not be distressed.' But he did say: 'Thou shalt not be overcome.'

You are the Christ

Aim

To encourage a personal relationship with Christ the living Lord.

Readings

Isaiah 11:1-5
Psalm 110:1-4
Acts 10:34-43
Mark 8:27-38

Thought for the day

Jesus and the disciples are 25 miles north of the Sea of Galilee in an area that was well known for pagan worship. They are travelling around the villages of Caesarea Philippi. This area was famous for the worship of the god Baal in ancient times. The Greeks said it was the birthplace of Pan, the god of nature: the pipes of Pan could be heard in the woods and wood nymphs were to be seen dancing. It was here that Herod the Great built a gleaming white temple for the worship of Caesar. Herod's son Philip beautified the temple and added his name to the town, so that it became known as Caesarea Philippi. It was here, most likely under a starry sky by a campfire, that Jesus asked the disciples about their thoughts towards him.

Jesus asks first, 'Who do people say that I am?' Some were saying he was John the Baptist returned from the dead. No doubt this caused some amusement in the camp. Others were saying he was Elijah returned to herald in the coming of the Messiah. Yet others were saying he was a prophet, a good man and a wonder-worker. People still suggest all sorts of ideas about who Jesus is.

Jesus then asks, 'But who do *you* say that I am?' This is what Jesus wants to know from each of us. Not a summary of other people's ideas. He wants the reply from those who have spent time with him, the personal conviction of a disciple. It is not enough to be able to recite creeds or what others have said about Jesus. A person can be an atheist and still pass exams in theology. You can be able to recite stories about the historical Jesus and not be a Christian. Jesus seeks a personal response from each of us. He wants us to know him, to talk to him, and only then talk *about* him. Notice how personal Jesus is in his invitations:

Come to me.
I will refresh you.
Abide in me and I will abide in you.

We can only be true disciples if we spend time with him, if we get to know him. Then we can respond as Peter does by saying, 'You are the Christ, the Messiah.' When we personally come to know Jesus as the 'Anointed One of God' we will acknowledge him as our Lord and Saviour. One of the reasons Jesus told the disciples to tell no one is that people had wrong ideas about what the Messiah should do. They would learn through Jesus that being the Messiah would involve his suffering, and they would discover that they will be called to suffer like him.

Peter tried to sway Jesus away from any conflict but Jesus knew he could not escape the battle if he had come to win people to God. He knew the powers of evil would rally against him and he could not run away. He did not want to suffer; that's what made Peter's words all the more dangerous. The Tempter often seeks to weaken our resolve through our friends. We need to learn to stand firm.

Illustration

In his poem 'Gareth and Lynette', Tennyson tells of the struggle Gareth has to leave home. He wants to become one of the knights of Arthur but his mother does not want him to leave home. She has already lost two of her sons to Arthur's court. 'Hast thou no pity on my loneliness?' she asks. 'Stay, my best son, ye are yet more a boy than a man,' she pleads. The mother produces excellent reasons for Gareth to stay at home and ignore his vision. Here, the tempter is using someone who loves him dearly to stop Gareth serving his vision. Gareth replies:

O Mother,
How can you keep me tethered to you – Shame.
A grown man I am, a man's work I must do.
Follow the deer? Follow Christ the King,
Live pure, speak true, right wrong, follow the King –
Else, wherefore born.

Gareth was not tempted through his mother but followed the vision as he saw it.

In the same way Jesus could not allow Peter to sway him from his purpose.

Death Bears Fruit

Aim

To look at the Passion of Christ and beyond to the resurrection.

Readings

Isaiah 50:4-10
Psalm 31:9-16
Hebrews 5:5-10
John 12:20-33

Thought for the day

Philip told Andrew about some Greeks wanting to see Jesus. Andrew in his usual fashion brings them to Jesus. Here were seekers who were not Jews coming to meet the Saviour. It was an exciting moment. Jesus increases the excitement by saying, 'The hour has come for the Son of Man to be glorified.' The disciples would see this as the coming of the promised kingdom of God. This was exciting indeed. So the next words came as a shock as Jesus started to talk of death. He told them how troubled his soul was. Like any human being he did not want to die. He was only 33 years old; he did not seek out death. But he came to do whatever was the will of the Father.

For grains of wheat to grow, their burial is necessary. Only by death comes new life. If we hide the grain in a box to keep it safe and secure, it will be useless. Only when it is put in the cold earth can it rise to new life. Only by giving it away to the earth can we receive a good return.

Often we seek comfort and safety. We avoid conflict or having to put ourselves out. We look after ourselves. Jesus tells us that anyone who hoards their life or their talent will lose it. It is no use just surviving; we need to live life to the full. This will involve risk and danger. But of life it can be said: 'Use it or lose it.'

Bearing in mind what the world did to Jesus, whoever wants to serve him must realise they will not escape from similar troubles.

Today we end with a vision of the future. When Jesus has triumphed over the rulers of this world. 'When I am lifted up from the earth, I will draw all people to myself.' Looking back through two millennia, we can see how the cross has drawn all nations to come before him. We come to him who understands our suffering, who has borne our grief and our sins. We come to him who has triumphed over evil and through death opened to us the way to eternal life.

Illustration

Lazy Jack was given a sack of grain. His task was to sow the seed for the village so that they would have a harvest in the autumn. Jack looked at the seed. It was golden and beautiful. He thought it would be a shame to bury it in the ground. So he took it home and put it in a cupboard. No one knew that he had not sown the seed. Jack took it easy. It was only later in the year when there were no shoots, no signs of new wheat growing, that the village realised there was something wrong. Obviously the seed was not in the ground. After a search they found it in Lazy Jack's cupboard. The mice had eaten some, but most of it was still intact. Jack had almost allowed a community to starve by not sowing the seed. Like much in our lives, it was a case of use it or lose it. The villagers put the seed in the ground – it was late for sowing but they trusted in the power within the seed to grow and it did. In the end nothing was lost and the harvest was good.

The Servant King

Aim

To compare the ambition of James and John and the servant role of Jesus.

Readings

Isaiah 53:4-12
Psalm 18:1-6, 46-50
1 Peter 2:18-25
Mark 10:35-45

Thought for the day

Jesus is on his way to Jerusalem. He has turned towards the opposition, towards the cross and death. He wants his disciples to understand and be prepared. It must have been so hard for Jesus when they failed to grasp what he was saying.

James and John had just heard Jesus talking about his death and yet they were still thinking in terms of power and rule. They still did not understand what sort of Messiah Jesus is. They could only think in earthly terms. Only after the crucifixion would they see in a different way.

James and John were after position and promotion: they wanted personal gain and power. Their thoughts were on getting not giving, on success rather than sacrifice. The other ten disciples were angry with James and John because they thought they had tried to steal a lead on them. The twelve could only see the rule of Jesus and his kingdom in earthly terms of power and force. The Messiah the Jews hoped for was the Lion of Judah, a king like David who would drive out their enemies.

In today's reading from Isaiah we get a glimpse of a different Messiah: not so much the Lion of Judah but the Lamb of God. We see the portrayal of the Suffering Servant who gives his life for the sins of the world.

Jesus wanted the disciples to understand that he is about to fulfil the role of the Suffering Servant (see Mark 10:32-34). There may be a triumphal entry but soon the road will lead to the cross. Jesus did not come to win by force or to wield power. He came to win by love and to give his life as a ransom for many. Jesus could call on all the power and might that he desired but he chose the way of self-giving and love. Jesus understood you cannot force people into the kingdom, you cannot make people love God; you can only win them by love and grace. It is for this reason he calls his followers to do as he does, to give of themselves and to serve. A Christian can be seen as someone who has come down in the world. We should be able to step off our pedestal, relinquish our hold on power and possessions, and give ourselves in love and service. The question will not be how much you have gained but rather how much you have given of yourself.

The church that wields power and strives for position, that is full of pomp and possessions, is in danger of betraying the Servant King.

Illustration

When Toyohiko Kagawa, who lived in Japan, met Christianity he was captured by its call to serve. He prayed, 'O God, make me like Christ.' To become like Christ he went to live in the slums of Kobe to care for others. He chose to live in a shed that was about two metres square. On the very first night he was asked to share his room and bed with a man with a contagious itch, the first test of his aim to serve. He welcomed the poor man. Then a beggar asked for his shirt and he gave it. The next day the beggar came back for Kagawa's coat and trousers. Kagawa gave them and was left wearing a ragged kimono. At first the slum dwellers laughed at him but they soon came to admire him. Kagawa wrote:

> God dwells in the lowliest of men. He sits on the dust heap among the prison convicts. He stands with the juvenile delinquents. He is there with the beggars. He is among the sick; he stands with the unemployed. Therefore let him who would meet God visit the prison cell before going to the temple. Before he goes to church let him visit the hospital. Before he reads the Bible let him visit the beggar.

Palm Sunday

Aim
To share in the joy of the triumphal entry into Jerusalem, and in the sorrow for the events that followed.

Readings
Zechariah 9:9-10
Psalm 118:1-2, 19-29
Philippians 2:5-11
Mark 11:1-11 or John 12:12-16

Thought for the day
It would seem that Jesus had planned ahead for this visit to Jerusalem. The donkey was where Jesus said and the password 'The Lord needs it' would allow the disciples to take it. The fact that the colt had never been ridden made it especially suitable for religious purposes. The cart on which the ark of the Lord was carried had never been used for any other purpose (1 Samuel 6:7).

Jesus was received like a king as he approached Jerusalem. People spread their cloaks in front of him. This is what the friends of Jehu had done when he was proclaimed king (2 Kings 9:13). People waved palm branches as they did when Simon Maccabaeus came to Jerusalem after a great victory (1 Maccabees 13:51). The words of welcome came from today's Psalm 118, which was used to welcome pilgrims to the feast. The word 'Hosanna' means 'Save us now': people used it when addressing their king or their God.

The prophet Zechariah talked of the king to come entering Jerusalem upon an ass. Jesus is fulfilling a Messianic prophecy. The ass was seen as a noble animal but not an animal to ride to war with. Jesus was coming to conquer but with love and not by force. The ass was seen as an animal of peace and Jesus enters in peace. He comes not to destroy or condemn but to set free and to encourage. He will not force himself upon the people: love will be his restraint. In the days ahead we will see how people edge him out of their lives, out of their city and out of their world. We need to welcome him into our lives and into the world in which we move.

(Dramatic readings of the Bible texts replace the Illustration.)

EASTER
Easter Sunday

Aim

To rejoice in the resurrection and in the presence of the risen Lord.

Readings

Isaiah 25:6-9
Psalm 118:15-24
1 Corinthians 15:1-11
John 20:1-18

Thought for the day

Regularly someone will say, 'I would believe in the resurrection if someone came back from the dead.' Well, today we rejoice because someone has. Christ is risen. Alleluia!

Let Mary Magdalene and Peter tell their story. (Have three voices – Mary, Peter and Jesus.)

Mary starts.

I had another sleepless night. My eyes are red with crying. One of those nights when the darkness seems to last for ever. When Jesus died something in me died also; it was all so cruel. He forgave me my many sins, he loved me dearly and now he is dead. There is a weight on my heart like a heavy stone; like the stone rolled on to the tomb. Such a weight, for I saw him die, I saw his agony, I saw him deserted by his friends. It turned my heart to stone. Who can lift the stone from my heart? Jesus could but he is dead and a stone is rolled against his tomb.

I will go and be beside him. It is still dark – it is about 5am – but I will go. If only someone would roll the stone away.

Please, God, lift the stone from my heart and from the tomb.

O Lord! Somebody has been here, somebody with great strength. The stone has been moved. I will go and see my Lord. Oh no! They have taken away my Lord. They have stolen his body. O Lord, what have they done? I will go and tell Peter.

Let Peter take up the story.
I haven't cried in years. I do not like to see grown men cry. I am so ashamed of myself. How can I forgive myself? I said that I did not know Jesus; I denied him . . . At about 5.30 there was a banging on the door . . .

I was afraid. Then I realised it was Mary Magdalene, shouting and weeping. I could hardly get any sense out of her. She kept saying, 'They have taken away my Lord.' Young John and I were quickly on the road, running to the tomb. I am not as young as I used to be and John got there first. But he did not go in. I went in and saw the grave clothes discarded but there was no body. It was the way the clothes were wrapped that was odd; it looked as if he had just vanished from them or come through them. John came in and later he said, 'The empty grave clothes convinced me he had risen.' But at that moment we went back home. We passed Mary on the way.

Mary continues the story.
I went back hoping to find someone who had moved him. But I could not see for tears. I cried and asked aloud, 'Where is he?' . . .

But I must get a grip of myself. My vision is blurred. My heart aches. (*Jesus joins Mary)* Who is this? Is it the gardener? He seems to be looking at the spring flowers that have burst into life. Sir, they have taken away my Lord. Do you know . . .

'Mary.'

No, it can't be! Is it really you? This is madness.

'Mary.'

It is you! Jesus, it really is you!

'Mary.'
Master, Master. Let me stay here close to you. Let me hug you and be with you for ever.

'Mary, do not cling to me. You cannot keep me to yourself. You will have to let me go. You will have to go, Mary. Go and tell the disciples that I am alive, I am risen. Tell them you have seen me.'

I did not want to go but he asked me. I ran again to the house and told the disciples, 'I have seen the Lord! Alleluia!'

Illustration

Napoleon escaped from his island prison. His armies regathered under the French flag and Europe was plunged into war. The British army under Wellington landed in Belgium and prepared to fight near a small village called Waterloo. There was no way of communicating to England the news except by semaphore. Day after day a man watched from the tower of Winchester Cathedral, peering towards the south coast. On a misty day the watcher received a message: 'Wellington defeated.' The mist came down and a sadness filled Winchester and spread over England. The watcher stayed at his post. After a long while the mist lifted and the message was repeated: 'Wellington defeated.' But now two more words were added and they made a great difference: 'Wellington defeated the French.' The assumed defeat was a victory. A new message sped to London. Bells rang out and flags flew. The message, which seemed one of defeat, was in fact the start of the news of victory. Likewise we must move from the crucifixion to the joy of the resurrection. We are able to proclaim, 'Death is conquered. We are free. Christ has won the victory.'

Jesus Is Alive 1

Aim

To share in the wonder of the resurrection.

Readings

Acts 4:32-35
Psalm 133
1 John 1:1–2:2
John 20:19-29

Thought for the day

The disciples were locked in through fear. The room they were in was like the tomb; they were sealed in and afraid to venture out. They had lost their Lord and leader. They felt powerless, lifeless. How often do we feel like this, locked in and unable to do what we ought to do? Then Jesus came. There was no fuss. Suddenly he was there, alive and well. He greeted them as normal: 'Shalom. Peace be with you.' But this was a new peace, for the risen Lord offered it to them. He showed them his hands and his side (interesting to note not his feet; feet were usually bound to the cross and not nailed). 'Then were the disciples glad when they saw the Lord' must be one of the great understatements of the Scriptures. What joy, what wonder must have been theirs. Then Jesus again said, 'Peace be with you.' Jesus said that as God sent him out, he would send them out.

Jesus needs disciples to continue his work. He will work in them and through them but he needs disciples. Think on these words concerning the risen Lord by St Teresa of Avila:

> Christ has no hands, but your hands
> to do his work today.
> Christ has no feet but your feet
> to speed men on his way.
> Christ has no lips but your lips
> to tell men why he died.
> Christ has no love but your love
> to win men to his side.

We are called to be Christ to others and to see Christ in others. This is only possible if we are filled with his Spirit. Jesus breathed on his disciples. There can be little doubt the Gospel writer saw this as a new creation. With the resurrection, a new world was dawning for us all. It is his Spirit that equips us for the work we need do. It is not in book learning but in the power of his Spirit that we are able to go out in mission.

This happened to ten disciples; Judas was already dead and Thomas was away from the company. When Thomas was told, he refused to believe. Faith can be handed down but it must become first-hand for us. We need a relationship with the risen Lord. Thomas wanted to experience this wonderful event for himself. But to do it he stayed with the fellowship of the faithful. Jesus came again. Again we hear the words, 'Peace be with you.' Thomas is invited to touch and feel; this is no ghost – Jesus bears the marks of the crucifixion. Then Jesus says, 'Blessed are those who have not seen and yet have come to believe.'

Illustration

Suddenly a man fell to the ground. He had stopped breathing and it would not be long before he was totally dead. But help was at hand. Someone was willing to give him mouth-to-mouth resuscitation. They breathed their breath into him, filling his lungs, and then helped his lungs to expel the air and then receive some more breath. This process went on for a while at ten breaths a minute; without it the man would have died. By the time the ambulance came the man was breathing freely on his own. The person had saved his life. Jesus breathes new life into us and gives us eternal life. Jesus defeats death and brings us to eternal life.

(You may be able to get a St John's Ambulance person or a paramedic to offer to demonstrate 'Breath of Life' – they also provide a useful card with this title.)

Jesus Is Alive 2

Aim

To rejoice in the presence of the risen Lord.

Readings

Acts 3:12-19
Psalm 4
1 John 3:1-7
Luke 24:36-48

Thought for the day

Two of our readings today come from the writings of St Luke. He wrote the Acts of the Apostles as well as the Gospel according to St Luke. In Acts we hear of Peter telling his fellow Jews that the power he has comes from Jesus, whom they killed and God raised from the dead. Peter tells how the disciples are witnesses to the risen Lord. He invites the people to repent and to turn to God, just as Jesus asked him to do. The change in the disciples, from locked in and fearful men to being men willing to die for the Gospel, is the great proof of the resurrection. Peter points out that it is not in their power but in the power of the Lord that they are able to heal the lame man.

Luke's account of Easter Day differs slightly from the account of Mark and Matthew. Interestingly, Luke has the eleven disciples together (did he not know the Thomas story?). He also tells us of 'companions' being present: here is a brief insight into the fact that there were others and not all male. Suddenly Jesus is there among them, saying, 'Peace be with you.' This was the group that knew all about the crucifixion and burial – they had seen him die. They had watched his burial. Now they were startled and terrified for they thought it must be a ghost. Jesus tells them not to be afraid or doubting. It is Luke who mentions the feet of Jesus when Jesus invites the people to touch him and to look at his hands and feet. He wants them to know he is solid. Yet they still found it hard to believe. Jesus had to deal with them quite gently. He asked for something to eat and they gave him some fish. Ghosts do not eat. Jesus ate the fish in their presence.

Only when they are more relaxed does Jesus talk to them of

the prophecies in the Scriptures, of how the Messiah would suffer and rise from the dead. They are to proclaim repentance and forgiveness of sins. They are to be his witnesses. St John, in today's second reading, witnesses and calls for awareness that we are children of God and so we should turn away from evil and turn to God.

Illustration

Have you ever been caught in the fog? The whole world becomes cold and grey. Vision is greatly restricted. Everything around appears to be dull and damp. Then suddenly there is a shining, an extra amount of light; there is a radiance that begins to appear all around. The sun breaks through and the fog lifts and disappears. The day seems so glorious and bright. This was the experience of the disciples with the resurrection. They shut themselves in and shut the fullness of life out. They were locked in by sorrow and fear. They just wanted to hide. It was then he came. He came because he was needed. He came back from the dead. He came to be with them. He came to guide them. He came to help them. He came to be friends. He came to transform their world. He comes now and he comes to us. He comes to chase away our darkness and fear and to make our world bright.

JESUS AND HIS PEOPLE
The Vine

Aim
To show we are one with Christ and that we are called to bear fruit.

Readings
Acts 8:26-40
Psalm 22:25-31
1 John 4:7-21
John 15:1-8

Thought for the day
The vine was one of the most common plants in Israel. It would grow almost anywhere: it grew on walls, up trellises, around the doors of houses; it grew up sticks. It also grew in the wild. For the vine to grow well, it needed the ground to be prepared carefully and it needed regular attention. If you wanted good fruit, you could not just leave it to chance.

Could it be that with Jesus who says, 'I am the vine', we need to give the same attention? There is no one in whom he will not grow if only the preparation of the 'soil' is properly done. Today we expect instant results, instant responses, instant changes in people, instant conversions, and they do not happen because we ignore what is going on at ground level. We tend to ignore the weeds, the poor environment, the lack of sustenance; we want growth without having to make an effort.

Let us learn from the preparation of the vine. First it is necessary to prepare the ground, to see that the atmosphere is as good as possible for growth. We need to be sure that it will not be choked by weeds or die from lack of attention. Many who are young in the faith are lost because we do not give them the sustenance they need. It is lovely when growth begins. For a long time it seems little is happening and then suddenly growth speeds up. The vine is so luxuriant in its growth that young slips are usually set at two metres apart: to have room to grow is important. In the first three years the vine is not allowed to fruit so that it can conserve its life and energy. We often send people out before they have grown, and so they exhaust themselves and their fruiting is lost. Too often we rush young Christians into action, and they expect it, when we have spent little time building them up in the faith. We need those who are mature in the faith and who have the resources for bearing fruit.

The vine has two kinds of branches: one is fruit-bearing and the other is not. The non-fruit-bearing branches are drastically cut off so that they will not take away energy and strength from the plant. The vine will not produce a good crop without pruning. We are all meant to bear fruit in one way or another.

Lastly, though of utmost importance, we need to note that Jesus says he is the whole vine and we are the branches. We are not separate from Jesus. Without him we cannot bear fruit. But we are not without him. In fact, we dwell in him and he is in us. Without him, our lives will wither and die. If we abide in him and he in us, his life flows in us and through us. We are one with him and one in him. Then, in turn, we are the vine and we are called to be Christ to the world.

Illustration

We hear little of the disciples after the resurrection but we know they all bore the fruit of being with Jesus. After the death of Stephen, the disciples scattered because of persecution. We know Philip went to Samaria and told the story of Jesus. He preached of the love of God. Through the disciples the Church was growing rapidly and beyond the boundaries of Jerusalem (see Acts 8:4+). Peter and John also went to the Samaritans.

A road from Jerusalem went by Bethlehem and, just south of Gaza, joined the main road to Egypt and beyond. St Luke points out that this is the Old or Desert Gaza, not the more modern one. Along this road travelled the Chancellor of the Exchequer of the queen of Ethiopia. He had been to Jerusalem to worship. He is at least a seeker of God. He was in his chariot reading Isaiah 53. Philip simply asked if he understood what he was reading. The Ethiopian said how could he without a guide? Philip was invited into the chariot and they looked at the words: 'He was led like a lamb to the slaughter.' Philip talked of Jesus of the crucifixion and resurrection. The Ethiopian was moved and wanted to be baptised in the nearby water. After being baptised the Ethiopian went on his way rejoicing. Again we see Philip bearing fruit as he does the work of Jesus. Tradition has it that the Ethiopian went home and started to evangelise Ethiopia. And through the witness of many the Church grew in the faith and in number.

Friends

Aim

To know that we are chosen by God.

Readings

Acts 10:44-48
Psalm 98
1 John 5:1-6
John 15:9-17

Thought for the day

Have you ever been chosen to play for a team or to represent your school or firm? You are chosen because you can do certain things. You do not choose but you are chosen. You can try to earn a place but you cannot choose to be in the team. You are chosen.

A lot of people talk about choosing to be a Christian or not as if the choice was theirs. The choice is not ours; it is Jesus who chooses us. Jesus says, 'You did not choose me but I chose you.' We are asked to respond by saying whether or not we want to be part of his ministry and have a relationship with him. Any who excuse themselves exclude themselves.

Out of his love and grace God has called us. In today's Gospel we can see what that calling implies.

(1) We are chosen for joy. No matter which way the road goes, whether life is tough or easy, we are called to rejoice in the Lord (see Philippians 4:4). The Christian is a person of joy, knowing that God calls them and knowing that the Lord is with them. This is a joy no one or nothing should be able to take from us. Amidst all the gloom a Christian is to show joy, for we are loved and have an eternal destiny.

(2) We are chosen for love. Jesus gives to us an awareness of the love of the Father. He gives us his own love. What greater love can he give us than laying down his life for us? Jesus demonstrated his deep love for us on the cross. We are called to respond to this love by loving him. Then he has chosen us to love one another as he loves us. 'This is my commandment, that you love one another as I have loved you.' Warring factions among Christians betray the love of Christ.

(3) We are chosen to be friends of Jesus: 'I do not call you servants (slaves) any longer.' It was counted a great honour to be called slaves or servants of God. Moses was called the 'slave of God' (Deuteronomy 34:5); so was Joshua (Joshua 24:29); so was David (Psalm 89:20). St Paul also was proud to call himself a slave (Titus 1:1). One of the titles of the Pope is 'Servant of the servants of God'. But Jesus has called us to a far greater privilege: we are to be his friends and friends of God. We need not stand far off; we have immediate access to the presence of our friend. We are not like someone who gets a rare glimpse of the king; we are able to enter into his presence whenever we want. He has chosen us to be his friends. Because Jesus is alive he is not a theory or an idea; he is a person. We need to talk to him and make friends with him.

As always, with privileges come responsibilities. We have been chosen to 'go': Jesus sends us (in the way some are 'sent' by their favourite pop star). We need to learn to 'go for Jesus'. We are all called to share in the outreach and mission of our Lord.

We are called to bear lasting fruit, to be ambassadors for Christ. We are to show by our way of living that it is a joy to be a friend of God and to love as he loves us. We are his witnesses and witnesses to the riches of his glory. We are advertisements to our God and his love – or we ought to be.

To be able to do all this we are asked to pray to the Father in the power of Jesus. We cannot achieve this work in our own strength but only in the power and presence of God.

Illustration

Once upon a time there was an explosion that radiated out through the world. Countless people were touched, infected: many found it contagious as someone who was already touched passed it on to them. The explosion happened on a hill called Calvary just outside Jerusalem. Here love broke out in great power, defeating darkness. In a flash of blinding love, the Christ released a new way of life for the world. The love of God radiated through the whole earth and all times. The results of that explosion are still being felt today because he who died rose again. He lives and seeks to share his love with us. He comes to us and wants to be our friend. There are always those who will protect themselves against such an event; who will ignore his presence and avoid his radiant love. But he will transform all who come to be touched and give them the power to become the true children of God. They will shine with his presence and his love.

One Church

Aim

To express the unity of all believers, as there is only 'One Church, one faith, one Lord'.

Readings

Numbers 11:21-29
Psalm 124
James 5:13-20
Mark 9:38-50
Matthew 5:13

Thought for the day

Pride and prejudice or a feeling of our own insecurity and uncertainty often make us set ourselves against others. We see people as rivals, when in reality they are seeking the same good that we are. Sadly, the history of the Church is often one of rivalry and bitter factions. We set rules and regulations to say we are special and suggest others are not, especially if they do things in a different way. Many a church is afraid of, or incapable of, change or taking on something new. There seems to be a built-in fear of anything different. This was often the trouble with the Scribes and Pharisees when they met Jesus: they could only accept Jesus on their terms; they could not see that he had anything to offer.

In today's Gospel, John expresses a feeling of being scandalised by an exorcist who was casting out demons in the name of Jesus. In the ancient world there was a universal belief in demons. Everyone believed that physical and mental illness was the work of demons. Anyone who was ill was under a malign influence. The commonest way to exorcise a demon was to find a more powerful spirit and command the demon in that name to come out of the person. The demon could not stand against a more powerful name. John had found a man driving out demons in the name of Jesus and had tried to stop him. The reason he gave was that he was not one of them – that is, the little company of men around Jesus. Jesus said the man should not be stopped. We need to learn that those who are not working against us are for us.

We need to learn there are more ways than we can understand

in which God comes to us and we come to God. We should not stop anyone because it is not our way. God is far bigger than our little understanding and works in many ways. We must guard against being exclusive. Heed these words:

> He drew a circle that shut me out –
> Rebel, heretic, a thing to flout.
> But love and I had the wit to win;
> We drew a circle that took him in.
> *Edward Markham (1852-1940)*

Let us rejoice in the other churches that are around us and in the work they do.

Illustration

Hospitality was of great importance in the ancient world. By being open to others, the great Other, who is God, was given the opportunity to enter into your life. See the example of Abraham and Sarah when visited by the Lord (Genesis 18:1-15). In the story it is hard to decide whether we are dealing with three men, three angels or the three-person God. Ask the congregation who visited Abraham: was it men, angels, God? (Be careful how you phrase the question for it is not an 'either/or'. All visited Abraham at Mamre. The person that replies 'Yes' to the question or says, 'All three' would get top marks!)

There is a Celtic poem which expresses the Other approaching us through others.

> I saw a stranger yestere'en
> I put food in the eating place,
> drink in the drinking place,
> music in the listening place
> and in the sacred name of the Triune
> he blessed myself and my house,
> my cattle and my dear ones,
> and the lark said in her song
> often, often, often,
> goes the Christ in a stranger's guise.

ASCENSION
Choosing an Apostle

Aim

To show the importance of knowing Jesus personally.

Readings

Acts 1:6-9, 15-17, 20-26
Psalm 24
Ephesians 1:15-23
John 17:6-19

Thought for the day

If you had to help to choose your next priest or minister, what qualifications would you look for? In some parishes it is easy: they look for an Oxford or Cambridge graduate only. That would weed out an awful lot. We want a learned man, but is intellect of the prime importance? A degree in theology may impress but it does not guarantee that the owner is a committed Christian! There is a big distinction between knowing about Jesus and knowing Jesus.

The disciples had to face this problem with the death of Judas. They were used to working as a team. They went in twos: rarely did they work alone. So eleven was definitely an odd number. Twelve is a special number, like the twelve prophets or the twelve tribes of Israel. If the apostles were like the new Israel they would need to make up their team to twelve. If we play with a team member short, it will affect our overall performance. They needed to find a replacement, so they got together and asked what was required. It is worth noting that at this stage there were about 120 gathered together – that could be ten for every apostle.

They decided together it should be someone who had been with Jesus from the beginning, from the baptism of John until Jesus was taken up from them. (Here we discover there were more than just the twelve going around with Jesus, but nevertheless twelve is a special number.) Then they would require that person to witness with them to the resurrection. Definitely called as a team member and definitely called to witness to the resurrection.

If they were able to put an advert in Situations Vacant it might sound like this:

> Due to the untimely death of an apostle,
> one person needed to join a team of twelve.
> Will normally be required to work with others.
> Needs to know Jesus personally
> and to be ready to witness to the resurrection.

The important things became obvious. They wanted someone who knew Jesus, not someone who had just heard of him. The person had to have followed and loved Jesus. What mattered was their personal experience of the Lord.

What would such a man see as his work?

Take services, look after churches, do social work? Above all he would have to witness to the resurrection. He would have to show others that Jesus is alive. Jesus is not a figure of history or just a holy man of the past: he *is* the *Living Lord*. We need to know him in the present tense, to know him now.

There seemed two obvious candidates, Joseph and Matthias. Now the followers of Jesus wanted to show that it was God's choice, not theirs. They prayed, 'Lord, you know everyone's heart. Show us which one of these two you have chosen.' Then they cast lots. We may find this a little strange but they wanted the choice to be God's and in those days this was a natural way of seeking that choice. The names of the candidates were written on stones. They were then placed in a vessel and shaken until one stone fell out. He whose name fell out was the chosen one. In this case Matthias' name came out and he became apostle number 12.

Illustration

In the film *Oliver!*, Oliver Twist is in the poorhouse with many other young people. They want someone to complain that they are hungry and want more food. In this case no one wants to do it for they know they are likely to be punished. They decided to pick straws and whoever draws the shortest straw has to do it. If you draw the shortest straw, it means you are chosen. Oliver draws the shortest straw. The others have elected him. So though he is frightened, he goes to the front and asks for more. 'Please Sir, I would like some more.' In the poorhouse this is unthinkable and, as the young people expected, Oliver is punished for asking.

PENTECOST
The Power of the Spirit

Aim
To rejoice in the presence and power of the Spirit.

Readings
Ezekiel 37:1-14
Psalm 104:24-34
Acts 2:1-12
John 15:26-27; 16:4b-15

Thought for the day
Today we lit the 12 candles and carried the 12 balloons to remind us what happened to the disciples at Pentecost. We heard in the Acts of the Apostles how there was a great wind that rushed through the house where they were, and that on each of the disciples there appeared to be tongues of fire.

Now here is something else to look at: it is a drill but it is useless (you could use anything that needs a power pack). It should be able to work but it does not. Who can tell me why it does not work? It could be that its batteries are flat or, like this one, it needs a power pack. Now if I snap this power into place, away it goes (demonstrate).

Pentecost was a time when all the Jews who lived near Jerusalem came to give thanks for the giving of the Law to Moses on Mount Sinai. It was also time to give thanks for the barley harvest. Pentecost was 50 days after the Passover, so for us it is 50 days after Easter. If you do not count Easter Day itself, it is only 49 days, 7 x 7, a week of weeks. Sometimes this was called the Festival of weeks.

The disciples were all together in a room. Perhaps they were still afraid to venture out. They did not show any signs of going out and talking about Jesus. In fact, they were waiting to be given the power. They had known Jesus; they had seen the risen Lord and they knew his presence in their lives. They had been commissioned by him to go out and preach the Gospel. But they were waiting for the power to go out. Jesus had foreseen this and had asked them to wait: 'Stay here in the city until you have been clothed with power from on high'(Luke 24:49). It was there, in the room where the disciples were, that the Spirit came with the sound of wind and tongues of fire. Wind and fire were symbols of great power in the ancient world and both were associated with the presence of God. Wind, breath and spirit were all linked together in the ancient world and all were signs of the Spirit of God.

Whatever happened, we know that on this day the disciples were empowered. They were given courage and the ability to go out and proclaim the Gospel. These 12 ordinary men were given the power that would transform the world. If we look at what they were like before the coming of the Spirit and what they were like after, we have proof that something great happened. They would all tell you the Spirit came. He comes to us too.

The Lord is here.
His Spirit is with us.

Illustration

One of Europe's leading ecologists has said the energy crisis we face is not so much in energy supplies but in our own thinking. There is enough energy in the ebb and flow of the tides, in the running of rivers, in the winds and in the rays of the sun to supply our needs if we would give time and attention to these. Three things are obvious:

(1) Many energy supplies are limited and will run out.

(2) Wrong thinking or lack of proper attention makes us do nothing.

(3) All around there is power that we do not realise.

Too often the Church tries to go along in its own resources and strength, and it can be seen to be running out of supplies. We spend too much of our attention looking in the wrong direction.

The power of God is here, for the Lord is here: His Spirit is with us.

We need to learn to wait upon the Lord and the power of his might.

TRINITY
A Balanced Idea of God

Aim

To encourage a greater awareness of the Trinity.

Readings

Isaiah 6:1-8
Psalm 29
Romans 8:12-17
John 3:1-17

Thought for the day

Do you have a proper diet? We do not all need to eat the same things but we do need a balanced diet. The body cannot live for long without the proper sustenance – fasting can be useful but starving yourself is useless. Many starving people get weak and disorientated. While most of us are not likely to starve, even a slight deficiency can reduce our well-being. A lack of calcium or iron or even zinc in their minute quantities can affect our health.

There was a farm that was not prospering. The cows were losing weight and dying. The family was being reduced to poverty. It seemed disaster was inevitable. Then the vet discovered a chemical deficiency in the cows' feed. The necessary chemical was added and, almost immediately, cows, farm and family improved.

Why are we talking about deficiency? It is because so many people are deficient in their Christian life; there is an element lacking and that leaves them poor when they should be rejoicing in the great riches that are offered to them. They have not experienced the Trinity: they have latched on to one of the persons of the Trinity and missed out on the other two. Quite often if you look at your prayers, you will discover you neglect to have a relationship with one of the three, either Father, Son or Holy Spirit. In the words of Saint Paul: 'The grace of the Lord Jesus Christ, the love of God, and the communion of the Holy Spirit be with you all' (2 Corinthians 13:13).

Check your own experience. Are you aware of a loving Creator who cares for his creation? Do you know he made you out of his love and for his love? He surrounds you with love and wants you to respond to him with love. Do you rejoice to know that nothing in this world can separate you from the love of God? He is with you, the Almighty, the Creator and seeks your love.

Have you discovered the grace – that is, the free gift and the beauty – of our Lord Jesus Christ? Know that he came to earth for you. He lived and died and rose again for you. You do not have to earn his love; it is a free gift (gratis). When you cannot help yourself, he comes to your aid. He is your Saviour and Redeemer. He loves you and he seeks your love.

Are you in common union – communion – with the Holy Spirit? He is with you at every encounter; he shares in every bond of fellowship. The Spirit brings gifts and talents for you to use. As last week, all need learn to wait upon the Spirit.

Father in heaven, you are our Creator.
Jesus, you are our Saviour.
Spirit, you are our Guide and Strengthener.

Make sure you know this and rejoice in Father, Son and Holy Spirit, in the Holy Trinity.

Illustration

A child went down to the beach and dug a hole in the sand. She then went down to the sea and brought some water to fill the hole. In a moment the water disappeared. She went back for more water, and then more. But the same thing happened each time. The little girl became exhausted and began to cry. Meanwhile the tide had been coming in. Her father showed her how to make a channel for the sea, so that it would flow naturally into the hole and fill it. We are like the little girl: we try to fill our minds with ideas about God and often exhaust ourselves. We talk too much. We need learn to wait upon God, knowing he will come to us. Trying to understand the Trinity is like trying to pour the whole sea into a small hole. Yet we can rest in the Trinity and enjoy the love of Father, Son and Holy Spirit.

JESUS HEALS 1
Healing and Prayer

Aim
To show the need for prayer.

Readings
Isaiah 40:21-31
Psalm 147:1-12, 20c
Acts 3:1-10
Mark 1:29-39

Thought for the day
Isaiah tells us that God is Almighty; that he gives power to the faint and strengthens the weary. There is no doubt of God's power and that he knows all that he has made. Then we are told 'those who wait for the Lord shall renew their strength'. We should all take these words to heart.

The psalm tells us though the Lord knows all the stars he is still concerned for us and heals the broken-hearted, and has pleasure in those who await his gracious favour. It would be good if we knew this in our lives.

In Mark's first chapter we get a glimpse of how busy Jesus was. On the day of rest he went to the synagogue. He taught with authority and healed the man who had an unclean spirit. At midday he went home with Simon Peter. Here Simon's mother-in-law had taken ill and was lying down with a burning fever. Jesus went to her and took her by the hand and raised her up. How many people does Jesus, the risen Lord, still take by the hand and help them to rise? Peter's mother-in-law immediately feels well and looks after her guests. There are two things to notice here. First, Peter is obviously married. The second is that the ministry of Jesus often depended on the care of such noble women as Peter's mother-in-law.

As it was the Sabbath, movement was restricted. When the sun went down a new day began. Because there were no clocks, it was said to be evening when three stars could be seen in the sky or when the last rays of sunlight had gone. The people waited patiently but were anxious not to miss Jesus. As soon as it was dark the streets were full of people coming to see Jesus and bringing the sick and indisposed with them. Often, in history, people come out of the darkness to him who is the Light of the World. It looked as if the whole of Capernaum had come out. Jesus must have looked after people well into the night and was probably exhausted.

Like any sensible person, Jesus knew he could not go on pouring out his energies without being renewed and refreshed. He needed new power. So, we are told, 'while it was still dark he got up and went out to a deserted place and prayed'. His ministry could only continue if he maintained a constant link with the Father. We often lack power and energy because we seek to go in our own strength. Remember the words of Isaiah: 'Those who wait for the Lord shall renew their strength.'

Jesus put himself out to get up extra early. Then he sought a place where he would have a time of quiet, and there he prayed. If Jesus felt the need to do this, there must be something wrong in our lives if we do not make time to pray.

Illustration

It is not often you see one of these in church – a battery charger. Sometimes, even when there is fuel in the tank, the engine will not start. This is because there is no spark, no electricity to fire the engine. Then you need the battery charger. It will slowly revive the flat battery and give it new life. Then we will be able to get going again. Also a car cannot run for long without being refuelled. You need to fill it up regularly with petrol. The more miles you do, the more petrol you need.

Some of you may have battery chargers at home to charge up batteries for CD players or other things that need electricity to keep them going. Many modern torches come with a charger so that the battery can produce a bright light.

Sometimes people are a bit like a beautiful car with a full tank of petrol but a flat battery. They should be able to do all sorts but they are flat and dull or feeling run down. So many seem to lack a bright spark in their lives. When this is so, we need power from outside ourselves. Listen again to Isaiah: 'Those who wait for the Lord shall renew their strength.'

Healing and Forgiveness

Aim

To show our God is a healing and forgiving God.

Readings

Isaiah 43:18-25
Psalm 41
2 Corinthians 1:18-22
Mark 2:1-12

Thought for the day

In the mind of the Jews at the time of Jesus there was a definite link between illness and sinfulness. If you were ill it was because God was punishing you for your sins. God was a stern God who often punished his people. Jesus came to show that God has always been a loving and forgiving God. A parent may not like what a child is doing but the parent will still love the child. God hates sin but it does not stop him loving the sinner. This love is a free gift; it is the grace and goodness of God towards us. We cannot earn this gift but we need to learn to accept it.

In the reading from Isaiah, God tells the people to realise he is active now and is doing new things. There will be rivers flowing in what was a desert. Though his people had forgotten him and sinned against him, God will forgive them and not hold their past sins against them.

The Psalmist asks God for forgiveness and healing; the two go together.

We are told Jesus was 'at home' in Capernaum, but at whose home? Was it Peter's or even the home of the writer of this Gospel? We are not told, but Jesus is at home. Are you sure Jesus is at home in your house?

Here in Capernaum Jesus healed the man in the synagogue, Simon's mother-in-law, and all those who came to him once the Sabbath was over. It is not surprising that crowds came again for teaching and healing. This time there were some scribes keeping an eye on Jesus and making sure he did the right thing.

Four men brought a paralysed friend to Jesus. When their way was barred by the crowds, they struggled on to the roof and broke through the plaster and brush wood. (Remember, the houses had flat roofs and outside stairs up to them.) Then they lowered the man. It is a wonderful action to bring people to Jesus.

Jesus looked at the man and said, 'Son, your sins are forgiven.' I am sure the man hoped for more but perhaps this had to be said first. The Scribes were annoyed because only God can forgive sins. Who did this Jesus think he was? Jesus could see what they were thinking and turned to the paralysed man and said, 'I say to you, stand up, take your mat and go to your home.' With those few words Jesus healed the paralysed man. If sin is portrayed as illness, surely if the man was healed he was also forgiven. This is another sign, a pointer to who Jesus really is. The people glorified God and said, 'We have never seen anything like this.' Let us be sure we have come before Jesus and found forgiveness and healing.

Illustration

What a wonderful hymn *'New every morning'* is; we need to take it to heart. Read verse 1. We are here awake and alive due to the love of God. During the night we have been refreshed and restored in our powers.

Read verse 2. This verse can change our lives if we take it to heart. 'New perils past': some of the things we feared yesterday did not happen or were not half as bad as we thought. 'New sins forgiven': you need to accept this. What wrongs you did before today are forgiven as long as you intend to lead a new life. You need not carry a great load of guilt around with you; guilt does not change the past but forgiveness changes the future. In the grace and goodness of God you are given a new day – learn to live it. Do not drag old sins and guilt around with you, for they will hamper your life. Start the day anew. Give thanks for the love and the healing power of God in your life. Know you are 'ransomed, healed, forgiven'. Start each day in the presence of God and with new hope in your heart: 'new thoughts of God, new hopes of heaven'.

The Authority of Jesus

Aim

To continue to show signs of the Christ.

Readings

Deuteronomy 18:14-20
Psalm 111
Revelation 12:7-12
Mark 1:21-28

Thought for the day

The people of Israel recognised the dangers of approaching such a powerful person as God. Being too close made them aware of their sinfulness and their mortality. They feared both the voice of God and the fire. They asked that someone stood between them and God. As light reveals darkness, so the presence of God can reveal our weakness and sinfulness.

If there is any evil in the world, and I am sure there is, we should expect it to cry out against or oppose goodness. Evil and God cannot exist side by side.

In Mark's Gospel we are shown Jesus at the beginning of his campaign. Jesus has received the Father's approval at his baptism. He has been tested by the devil and chosen the way he will take. Disciples have been selected. Now he must begin his campaign. As you might expect, we hear of his beginning in a church. People recognised a personal authority. But there was also opposition. The Church is made up of humans; it is not perfect, and it needs salvation. The man with the unclean spirit shouts out, 'What have you to do with us, Jesus of Nazareth? Have you come to destroy us? I know who you are, the Holy One of God.' Whatever you make of 'unclean spirits', for Jesus here is opposition. It is worth noting that the unclean spirits recognise Jesus; they know him. Knowing of Jesus is not enough. We are called to love him and obey him.

Here was confrontation, a testing time for Jesus. Talk is all right, but can Jesus produce the action to go with his words? There was even more at stake, for most believed that demons were so powerful that only God could cast them out. Did Jesus have the power? Jesus showed that even his words were powerful enough. It was not the man but the evil spirit Jesus addressed: 'Be silent and come out of him.' This was not a request but a command, and the spirit came howling out of the man.

The people were amazed; this was a new teaching with authority ('Whose authority?' we must ask). He commands even evil spirits and they obey him. (Surely only God can do that!)

We may find it hard to believe in evil spirits, yet there are many people who struggle against evil and disease, and have the feeling they are not dealing with something passive but with a cunning and resourceful enemy.

Jesus began his ministry in the synagogue at Capernaum and immediately his fame spread throughout all Galilee. But only some will see the signs pointing to Jesus as the Son of God.

Illustration

Show an array of lights.

An ordinary lamp is useful when the sun goes down for it helps us to see around the house in the dark. A torch is useful for it is the sort of light you can carry around with you and use whenever you need it. Laser light is used in hospitals for surgery and it is also used as a military weapon – laser always has to be used with great care. A security light is good to welcome you home and also to show up any intruders. People who like to sneak about in the dark do not like security lights – especially if linked with a burglar alarm.

The greatest light we have is the sun. Without the sun all life on earth would perish. We need the sun to survive. We also need it to see where we are going. Yet we cannot look directly at the sun and sometimes we cannot even stay in the sunshine without some protection.

In the same way, we cannot behold the full glory of God but Jesus reveals God to us.

Against the Rules?

Aim

To show that lives are richer than the keeping of rules – but that rules are necessary.

Readings

Deuteronomy 5:12-15
Psalm 81:1-10
2 Corinthians 4:5-12
Mark 2:23–3:6

Thought for the day

Self-righteous church people can be very frightening. They are usually full of negative goodness. 'I don't smoke, I don't drink, I don't chase after women (or men), I don't swear.' I want to ask, 'What do you do? What is your positive contribution to life?' It is sad when religion is portrayed as something that is life-restricting and negative. Jesus said, 'I came that they may have life and have it abundantly' (John 10:10).

In today's Gospel we meet religious people who are opposed to Jesus and his ways; in fact, they are out to kill him. We should not be surprised when we are faced with opposition as Christians: Jesus faced it throughout his ministry.

It begins in a cornfield. As the disciples were going through the field they plucked the ears of corn and ate them. It was all right to do this as long as they did not use a cutting instrument such as a sickle. Travellers were allowed to take and eat corn, but not on the Sabbath. Then it was not lawful because it was counted as work; in fact, it broke at least four rules of working on the Sabbath. The disciples could be accused of reaping, winnowing, threshing and preparing a meal! You wonder who was spying on them.

The Pharisees expected Jesus to tell his disciples not to do such things. In reality, the Pharisees were out to stop Jesus. If he gave in to this pettiness, he would hardly lead people to freedom. Jesus replied by telling them how David, when hungry, ate the sacred bread that only priests could eat (see 1 Samuel 21:1-6), citing this as a precedent for what the disciples were doing. Religion was not about rules and regulations but about a relationship with God. It is no use keeping the rules without a loving relationship. God wants our obedience but not as slaves. He wants us to do his will out of love. It would appear there was little love among these Pharisees.

The opposition continued in the synagogue. It is sad when a church reflects all too human feelings of violence and hatred. The Pharisees almost wanted Jesus to heal the ill man so that they could condemn him. Jesus does not play for safety. He could have healed the man after the Sabbath. He asks the man to come forward to let it be seen what he is doing. He faces the Pharisees and asks them, 'Is it lawful to do good or to do harm on the Sabbath, to save life or to kill?' Jesus had come to heal and to save; the Pharisees were plotting the death of Jesus. Such an attitude angered Jesus; he was saddened at their hardness of heart. Like Pharaoh dealing with Moses and the people of Israel, hardness of heart comes through regularly hardening ourselves.

Jesus heals, giving new life to the man with the withered hand. The Pharisees go out and make an unholy alliance with the Herodians. Normally, the Pharisees would have no dealings with the Herodians who were considered untouchable. Opposition mounts as members of government and church join forces to destroy Jesus. So often there are groups in our society that still seek to do this and we need be aware of it.

Illustration

Rules and regulations are there to help us and the society we live in. Occasionally you hear of some absurd application of the law, usually by someone who says something like, 'It's more than my job's worth.' A young motorcyclist was knocked off his bike in an area of parking meters. His bike was put carefully at the side of the road. Even though the traffic warden knew of the event, he placed a parking ticket on the bike. Fortunately, the city council was more understanding when a plea was made. Some people find it very hard to understand that rules are there to help us rather than hinder us.

FOLLOWING JESUS
Called

Aim

To show that God calls each of us and we all have an opportunity to answer that call.

Readings

Jonah 1:1-17; 2:10; 3:1-3
Psalm 148
Romans 8:28-30
Mark 1:14-20

Thought for the day

The Sea of Galilee is 13 miles long by 8 miles across at its widest from east to west. St Luke never calls it a sea but only a lake. The Sea of Galilee lies in the rift of the Jordan valley and is 680 feet below sea level. The Jordan flows into it in the north and out in the south going towards the Dead Sea. In the days of Jesus, Josephus, who was governor of Galilee for a while, tells us that there were about 330 fishing boats that sailed Galilee. Galilee had at least nine populous towns. Bethsaida, the home of Andrew, Peter, James and John, meant 'the house of nets'; another had the name of Tarichaea, the place of salt fish. People ate little meat and fish was their staple diet. Fish was salted to keep it fresh and it was exported from Galilee to Jerusalem and Rome.

There were three modes of fishing. The first used line, hook and bait. The second was with a drag net that had ropes at the four corners and was dragged behind a boat, or, more often, behind two boats. The third method was a casting net which was circular and up to about nine feet across. This net was skilfully cast from the shore or from a boat in shallow waters. It was a casting net that Simon and Andrew were using as Jesus passed along the shore.

Mark gives the impression of a call from out of nowhere, but if we read John 1:35-40 we discover Jesus had contact with the fishermen before today.

Jesus had talked to them. They had listened. What Jesus wanted now was not discussion but reaction. At this moment it was time for the talking to stop and for them to answer his call. Very often when God or Jesus calls, man stalls. See the story of Jonah. The first time God called Jonah and asked him to go east towards Iraq, Jonah set off in the opposite direction and went west towards Spain. If we turn a deaf ear to the call, it does get harder to hear, yet God still calls each of us. Vocation is not for some people only; God has a calling for everyone.

Fish must have often escaped and slipped through the net of the disciples. They often went out and caught nothing. Sometimes they must have seen great storms and thought, like the Breton fishermen, 'Lord, the sea is so large and our boat is so small.' Jesus wanted men who had learnt patience and perseverance, who were courageous and who knew the right time to 'fish'. Jesus wanted them to use their expertise and their talents in his service. The word Mark likes using, and he uses it about the reaction of Simon, Andrew, James and John, is 'immediately' . . . they followed him. If we put off following Jesus, it gets harder to do it later. There are times when we must be aware of the immediacy of the call.

Illustration

The need to react to God's call is caught well in Shakespeare's *Julius Caesar*, Act IV:

> There is a tide in the affairs of men,
> Which, taken at the flood leads on to fortune;
> Omitted, all the voyage of their life
> Is bound in shallows and in miseries.
> On such a full sea we are now afloat,
> And we must take the current when it serves,
> Or lose our ventures.

Fortunately, our God will call us again and again. There is a time when we have to stop talking about Christ and set out to follow him.

Jesus calls us, whoever we are.

There was once a very ordinary man (if there is such a being) called Aeshines, who came to Socrates and said, 'I am a poor man. I have nothing to give you but myself.' Socrates replied, 'Do you not see that you are giving me the most precious thing of all?'

Jesus wants the gift of ourselves far more than talk and theory Will we truly seek to follow him?

Different Responses

Aim

To show Jesus has work for us but will not force himself or his work upon us.

Readings

Ezekiel 2:1-5
Psalm 122
2 Corinthians 12:2-10
Mark 6:1-13

Thought for the day

Not everyone welcomed Jesus: that should be obvious from the crucifixion. Jesus was often scorned and rejected and not always popular. It is to be expected that if Jesus was not popular, then his disciples and followers would not be popular either.

Often what stops people accepting Jesus is their pride and prejudice. Jesus is not given a chance because people have made up their minds before they meet him.

It was quite natural for Jesus to turn up at Nazareth where he lived most of his life. He went to the synagogue and taught but the people could not hear him because of their prejudice. 'How can he preach? Is he not a carpenter? Let him get back to making furniture.' They saw Jesus as a craftsman, but could not see him as a preacher. They could see him as he was, but could not accept him for what he had become. He had changed but they were unwilling to. Sadly, some would think he could not have a great message because he was just a working man. Where did he get his wisdom from, for he was no scholar!

They knew his family, his mother Mary, his four brothers James and Joses, Judas and Simon, and his sisters. Here we get a glimpse of home at Nazareth. Jesus was not an only child. He grew up in what we would consider a large family. Joseph is not mentioned so it is likely he was dead. As Jesus was the first-born, he probably had to work hard to help to bring up this family, and that is why he is still at Nazareth until he is about 30 (Luke 3:3). The people who knew his family would not accept that Jesus could achieve anything special because he was so ordinary in their eyes, and so they rejected him. How can a carpenter preach? Such prejudice has hindered many a good man or woman. Even though Jesus cured some sick people, the people of Nazareth could not see his power. There is none so blind as those who do not want to see.

Jesus was amazed at their unbelief. He knew them and did not expect it from them. Before he left he said, 'Prophets are not without honour, except in their home town, and among their own kin, and in their own house.' This is a very sad statement from Jesus.

When people refuse to hear, Jesus moves on; he goes to other villages. Jesus never forces himself on anyone. We all have the choice to accept him as our Lord and our Friend or to ignore him. Many are not antagonistic to Jesus; they just cannot be bothered to put themselves out. When Jesus is ignored or rejected he will move on unless we call him back.

He also sent his disciples out in twos giving them some of his power over unclean spirits. They were to go out in his strength, not their own. They were to go out in faith without taking provisions, financial protection or the security of extra clothing. They were to travel light. Likewise, we do not need degrees or theological training; we do not need special qualifications. We need to know Jesus. We need to be sent by him. This is what makes an Apostolic Church: people who are called and sent by Jesus. They were not to take a collecting bag because they were to give rather than seek to receive. The Church needs money to survive but if raising money is its priority, it is giving out a wrong message. Like our God, we are to give more than we demand.

The disciples were not sent out to create a message. They went out as Christ's messengers; evangelists are 'good news tellers'. In a sense all are called to be 'angels' – that is, God's messengers. The mission of the disciples is to share in the mission of Jesus. 'As the Father has sent me, so I send you' (John 20:21).

The message of the disciples begins as Jesus began: 'Repent' (Mark 1:15). It is a call to turn around: turn around because you are going in the wrong direction. This is a call that disturbs, a call to be aware of where we are going and to accept that we can change.

The disciples revealed the mercy – the loving kindness – of God in bringing liberty and healing. Like Jesus, they were not to force themselves on anyone. God respects our freedom. 'If any place will not welcome you and they refuse to hear you, shake off the dust that is on your feet as a testimony against them' (Mark 6:11).

Illustration

In the totalitarian state you are not allowed free choice. You must do as you are told. If you do not open your door to the officials, it will be broken down. You cannot hide because they will seek you out and make you do what they want.

Jesus is different. He has the power but he will not force himself upon you. The choice is yours: he respects your free will. You can edge him out of your life and home if you so choose. You can be too busy to bother to keep in contact with him if you so desire. He will not force you.

If you look at Holman Hunt's picture you will see the door has not been opened for a long time. Jesus stands there knocking and waiting to bring his light upon those who live within. There is no means of opening the door from the outside. If he is to enter, you have to let him in. It is good to think of these words of Jesus every day: 'Behold, I stand at the door and knock' (Revelation 3:20).

Faithfulness

Aim
To encourage people to be faithful to their Lord.

Readings
Genesis 17:1-7
Psalm 119:17-32
Romans 7:21-25a
Mark 8:31-38

Thought for the day
Have you ever played 'Follow the leader'? It is fun when the leader is doing nice things and safe things, but you have to think twice if the leader starts to do things that are dangerous.

Jesus called the disciples to follow him. They left their homes and their work and went around the country with Jesus. It was a wonderful time of miracles and crowds following him. Life was a great adventure. When they were sitting around a campfire one evening, Jesus asked them if they knew who he really was. After a while Peter said, 'We know that you are the Anointed One of God. You are the Christ.' Peter was very excited about this because he believed Jesus was very popular and powerful. But Jesus warned them of the troubles ahead. He told them the elders, the chief priests and the scribes would reject him and that he would be killed. Jesus did not want to be killed but he knew if he did God's work he would face opposition. He knew that evil is always against goodness. Peter would not believe it. He took Jesus aside and told him it could not be so. Jesus wished it was not so but he knew trouble lay ahead. Peter was trying to persuade him to run away or hide or go somewhere else. Peter did this because he loved Jesus. Jesus saw that Satan was using Peter's love to tempt him. He spoke very strongly to his friend and said, 'Get behind me, Satan! For you are setting your mind not on divine things but on human.' We have to be careful that our friends do not lead us astray from what God wants us to do. Sometimes they cannot understand that we need to be willing to give up all to follow our Lord.

Jesus did not promise that following him would be easy. He

said there would be times when we would have to deny even our own desires. If we are following the crucified one, we too have to take up our cross. Jesus knew that some things are lost by being kept to ourselves. We lose the ability to play the piano or to do well at sport if we do not practise. Practice means denying ourselves the time to go out whenever we feel like it. To follow Jesus means discipline. There can be no discipling without discipline.

Illustration

When Columbanus wanted to go and serve God as a monk his mother was not pleased. She loved him dearly and was afraid that he was wasting his life. He had lots of talent and ability. He could be someone very important in Ireland. She talked to him and tried to dissuade him, but he knew God was calling him to leave home and serve him in a monastery. His mother tried all sorts of ways to stop him. Though she loved him dearly, she was acting for Satan. Columbanus got ready to go. His mother went to the door of the house and lay down in the doorway to stop him. Columbanus was very sorry to see his mother do this, but he carefully stepped over her and went to serve God wherever God called him. In time, Columbanus did wonderful work for God in France and Italy. For a moment it would have been easy to give in and stay at home.

JESUS HEALS 2
Only Believe

Aim
To show Jesus is the giver of hope and life to those who believe.

Readings
1 Kings 17:17-24
Lamentations 3:22-33
Acts 5:12-16; Mark 5:21-43

Thought for the day
Here are two sad stories, one of a young girl and the other of an older woman. It would seem the young girl was an only child. She would be the light of her parents' life, their joy and a living expression of their love. Now it would seem that light was about to go out. What darkness and pain it must have caused the loving parents that their child was so ill.

This young girl was 12. That is to say she had grown into a woman. In the land where Jesus lived when you were 12 years and a day you were counted as grown up and could even get married. (Maybe all the girls over 12 would like to stand for a moment.) Sadly, just as she should have been starting her adult life, she was going to die. Her father called doctors and healers but the girl could not be made well. He was desperate and that made him go to Jesus.

The man was called Jairus and he was the ruler of the synagogue. He was the administrator: he saw to the good running of the synagogue and to the list of who would take services and preach. He was an important man, respected and of good standing. Now he threw himself at the feet of a wandering preacher. No doubt he was not sure of Jesus and maybe even thought Jesus was a heretic, but he threw himself down before Jesus. He put aside any prejudice. He put aside any pride and begged repeatedly, 'My little daughter is at the point of death. Come lay your hands on her, so that she may be made well and live.' Jesus went with him immediately.

The crowds held up their progress. People were all around and seeking to see Jesus or hear him. It was a slow journey and suddenly Jesus stopped. Everyone stood still. Jesus turned and looked at the crowds and asked, 'Who touched me?' The disciples said, 'Look at the crowds. How can you ask such a question? Lots of people must have touched you.' But Jesus knew power had gone out from him to someone. He asked again, 'Who touched me?' and looked at the faces in the crowd. A woman came forward and confessed. She suffered from haemorrhages and should not even have been there. Any contact with people would render them unclean by the law. She should not have touched Jesus. Maybe she thought she could steal some power. It sounds as if she was rather superstitious but, whatever she was, she was desperate for healing. Jesus said to her, 'Daughter, your faith has made you well. Go in peace, and be healed of your disease.'

This was wonderful but it was a delay, and while Jesus was there a message came that the daughter of Jairus had died. Jesus looked at Jairus and said, 'Do not fear; only believe.' At the house the professional mourners were weeping and wailing, the flute players were playing sad songs. The girl was dead. Jesus said to them, 'The child is not dead but sleeping.' They didn't believe him and continued their wailing and crying. Jesus put everyone out of the house except the girl's parents. Then with Peter, James and John he went up to where the girl was and taking her by the hand he said to her, 'Talitha cum.' This was the local Aramaic language that the child would know; it meant, 'Little girl, get up.' Immediately, with Jesus holding her hands, she arose. Jesus told them not to tell anyone – they would know soon enough. The girl needed rest and food.

Illustration

How often do we lose contact with friends because we do not make the effort? To maintain a relationship with anyone we need to meet them and talk to them. If they are far away we can at least write, telephone or send an e-mail. A once-a-year Christmas card could hardly be called contact.

In a car the contacts give a vital spark that fires the engine. If the contacts are broken, the engine will not fire properly. Even if we have plenty of fuel and the battery is charged, the car will not go if there are no contacts at work.

When Jesus asks, 'Who touched me?' could you say, 'It was I, Lord'? Do you keep in proper contact with Jesus? When the woman touched him, power travelled from Jesus to her. We so often fail to achieve because we go it alone and do not touch base with Jesus.

Open to All

Aim

To encourage our church to be open and welcoming.

Readings

Isaiah 49:1-7
Psalm 146
James 2:1-13
Mark 7:24-37

Thought for the day

The Pharisees had declared Jesus and the disciples to be unclean. This was a way of banning them and any who had contact with them from their synagogues. Therefore it is not surprising that the stories following this event come from a non-Jewish area.

Tyre and Sidon are famed for their Phoenician sailors who were the first to navigate the seas by the stars. Tyre is 40 miles north of Capernaum and Sidon is 60 miles away. Both cities looked to the sea and overseas for their trade.

Jesus is in Gentile territory. Just as the Jews would not soil their lips with unwashed pots, so they avoided contact with the Gentiles for that would also make them unclean. As Jesus challenged the distinction between clean and unclean foods, he is now challenging the distinction between clean and unclean people. The Jewish people survived through their exclusiveness. Jesus wanted to show that the love of God is inclusive. The rest of the world, the Gentiles, also have a place in God's kingdom.

Whilst there, Jesus is approached by two Gentiles. A woman comes asking help for her daughter and a man who is deaf with an impediment in his speech is brought to Jesus. The woman was a Greek, and adding to this that she was a Syrophoenician evokes the idea of the fractiousness there was between the Jews and the people of Tyre. There was a definite animosity between these groups. Jesus takes no notice of this division.

When Jesus replies to her plea for help, 'Let the children be fed first, for it is not fair to take the children's food and throw it to the dogs', he would have found many a Jew rejoicing, for they use the term 'Gentile dogs' as a term of contempt. Jesus used a diminutive word for 'dog' to soften this and there is no doubt his voice did not imply his rejection of the woman. Israel may be 'first' but only first; many others from the rest of the world would also be fed with the 'Bread of Life'.

The woman had sought Jesus out, and now from the Greek-speaking area of the Decapolis they brought to Jesus a man who was deaf and had an impediment in his speech. Again Jesus is to offer the healing and love of God to this Gentile. Isaiah said that a sign of God's kingdom would be when 'the ears of the deaf (are) unstopped . . . and the tongue of the speechless sing for joy' (Isaiah 35:5-6). On a deeper level we need to consider the Jewish idea of hearing and speaking. Hearing was the most important sense because it was through hearing and speaking that the covenant was given. It was Israel who heard; the Gentiles were deaf. The Gentiles cannot hear the word of God or sing his praises. Once more Jesus challenges this view by accepting the man who is brought to him. Jesus acts out the miracle as the man would not hear the words. When Jesus says, 'Ephphatha' – that is, 'Be opened' – it can be a call not only to the man but also to the opening of the Gentiles to the Christ. The ears of the Gentiles are opened to the Word of God. The man, representing the Gentiles, zealously proclaims what Jesus has done. The response is 'He has done all things well; he even makes the deaf to hear and the mute to speak.' The whole world is being opened to the Christ. Let not the Church act in exclusive ways.

Illustration

There was once a very famous church. Every Sunday it was fashionable to go there and be seen. People came in their finery. Some of the most important people of the land attended it. The music and the choir were superb, the ordering of the service was of a very high standard; everything done was to the highest degree of excellence and in the best possible taste. For a good few Sundays a poorly dressed and shabby-looking person turned up at the door but was turned away for one reason or another. After a few weeks of trying to get in, the woman sat on the lowest step and prayed to God, 'Lord, why can I not get entrance into this church?' The Lord replied, 'My daughter, how do I know? I have been trying to get into this church for years.'

Jesus Opens Our Eyes

Aim

To show that Jesus opens our eyes to the reality of the world.

Readings

Job 42:1-6
Psalm 34:1-8, 19-22
Ephesians 5:8-14
Mark 10:46-52

Thought for the day

Jericho is the lowest town in the world at about 700 feet below sea level. Here Jesus meets two people who were counted among the lowest of the low – a blind beggar and Zacchaeus, an inspector of taxes.

Jesus is on his way to Jerusalem, which is 17 miles from Jericho. This last journey is uphill nearly all the way. The Son of David is coming to the city of David and neither will be the same again from this encounter. In just over a week Jesus of Nazareth will be crucified. But at the moment Jesus is passing by.

Bartimaeus sees this as a once-in-a-lifetime opportunity not to be missed. The people had come out to see the miracle worker, the Rabbi, the wandering preacher. Here is a man more perceptive than them all. He can see his own need and he can see an opportunity when it presents itself. With both eyes closed he can see what the crowds do not. Here among them is the Messiah, the Son of David. The crowds are blind to this fact and try to keep the blind man quiet. But the man knows his urgency and cries out, 'Jesus, Son of David, have mercy on me.'

Jesus stands still and says, 'Call him here.'

When he is called the man throws off his cloak; not to be hindered, he springs up and comes to Jesus.

Jesus asks, 'What do you want me to do for you?' We all feel the answer is obvious – but not Jesus. He does not offer a cure without the man pointing out his need: there is no prescription without talking to the patient. The Saviour meets each need personally.

The man's sight is restored and he then follows Jesus. He did not just come to get what he wanted and leave; he became a follower of Jesus.

One of the signs of the Messiah and the coming of God's kingdom would be the opening of the eyes of the blind (Isaiah 29:18; 35:5). Those who are saved will see properly (Isaiah 52:10). Sadly there is a blindness of those who do not see God (Isaiah 43:8; 56:10; 59: 9-10). Vision is about how we see the world and how we perceive our God. Without vision, people and nations perish (Proverbs 29:18).

One of the great moments of our life is when our eyes are suddenly opened and we see as if for the first time. We see a world that is full of wonder and mystery, and we see a world that is God-filled and not empty. Let us make these word of Origen ours: 'May the Lord touch our eyes, as he did those of the blind. Then we shall see in the visible things those that are invisible.'

Illustration

The comic character Mr Magoo is funny because he is short-sighted, though in real life he would be a tragic person. He walks across crocodiles thinking they are logs. He steps out of a window in high-rise flats just as a window cleaner's hoist reaches the window. He steps off the side of a pier as a boat pulls level alongside. He does not come to harm but he often leaves a trail of chaos and disaster behind him.

Can we see what is happening around us, to our communities and the way we are shaping the future? Or are we content to leave it in the hands of those who are blind to many of the finer things of life? If we allow the blind to lead us, will we not both fall into the ditch?

It is of extreme importance that we make sure we are led by men and women of vision. It is no use having a quick fix or a laugh now if we are destroying our future. Pray for vision for yourself and your leaders.

GOD'S WORLD AND ITS KING
Love and Respect

Aim
To show that our relationships are important.

Readings
Job 1:1; 2:1-10 or Genesis 2:18-24
Psalm 8
Romans 1:18-23
Mark 10:2-16

Thought for the day
In Genesis we hear that it is not good for a human to be alone. The Three Persons God values relationships and love. Human beings are to have a relationship with the world around them. We are put in charge of a world and we are accountable to the Creator for it. God created all out of his love and wants us to love it also. We are to express our relationship with God through our relationship with his creation. We have a responsibility to God for our use of and our sharing in creation. The human cannot survive alone and needs a helper and a partner. We are responsible for and to our partner in all our dealings. Through the love and understanding we share, with each other, we will grow in our love and understanding of God. Our relationship with God is expressed through our relationship with each other. If we do not treat each other with respect and the world with respect, it is not likely that we will respect God. In the same way, if we betray our God, we are as likely to betray each other! When our relationships break down it is bound to affect our relationship with God who loves us equally.

In Job we see a wife who feels deeply for her husband and his suffering. She suggests he should curse the Creator for what has happened to him. Obviously she underestimates his relationship of trust with God. Job understands that life in this world is not all sunshine and roses.

We disturb the relationship with creation when we act through selfishness and greed; by doing so we act irresponsibly. The destruction of so many creatures and plants in the name of so-called progress is a good example. What is happening to the rain forests and what is happening to the poor of our world are reflections of our relationships. There is a danger we just use people and creatures for our own gain, regardless of the results.

The most testing relationships are those we live with. It is said of a home that it is where we are treated the best and react the worst. Do not let that be true of us.

Relationships must be worked at, must be maintained. We must never take each other for granted, or deal with each other as if we had a servant or a slave. Relationships are meant always to reflect love. When our hearts are hardened we are already beginning a divorce, a break in our relationships. This is as true of neglecting our prayers as of taking each other for granted.

The disciples did not want to be bothered by the children or those who were bringing them. Jesus saw a desire for a relationship with himself and with the Father.

Illustration

Once a bird flying high overhead saw how our world was becoming polluted. The bird saw the rubbish dumped into the sea and fish struggling to survive, great tracts of land being robbed of trees, the ice-caps slowly melting. So it decided that it must tell the humans about what was happening. The first group would not listen – well, who would believe a bird! The next group were making good profits and did not want anything to be disturbed. A third group said they would happily talk about it for years. No one wanted to do anything. Yet the bird knew that all things were linked together. If the humans destroyed the environment, all the birds and all the animals would also suffer. Why were the humans so insensitive to their surroundings and to each other? The bird learnt that the humans had lost a sense of awe and wonder because they had broken their relationship with the Creator God. If they would not listen to the cries of creation, if they would not listen to the voice of God, they were not likely to hear a bird.

The Kingship of Christ

Aim

To show that Christ is King and seeks to rule in our hearts.

Readings

Daniel 7:9-10, 13-14
Psalm 93
Revelation 1:4b-8
John 18:33-37

Thought for the day

Jesus is brought before Pilate on charges of sedition, but Jesus does not look like a leader of a serious revolution. (How wrong Pilate was!) Jesus looks far more like a peasant. As yet the charge had not been made, so Pilate questions the prisoner: 'Are you the King of the Jews?' The question is asked with a tone of derision, implying that he surely could not be. Pilate cannot accept the idea. Jesus replies by asking how Pilate has come to ask this, as this was not the charge against him. Who had suggested this to him? 'Do you ask this on your own, or did others tell you about me?'

Pilate shows contempt for the Jews: he is not one of this despised race but a Roman, whereas Jesus is a Jew and his own people have brought him to this. He can hardly be their leader. 'What have you done?'

In reply Jesus talks of his kingdom that is not of this world. Not of this world's way of thinking or acting. If it were, his disciples would surely be fighting to rescue him. But a kingdom of love cannot use force to gain its ends. It is love that will keep Jesus on this track and on the cross, not weakness or lack of power. The kingdom of Jesus is the one that captures hearts and wills.

Pilate does not understand this talk of other-worldly kingdom and asks, 'So you are a king?' To this Jesus cannot answer because of Pilate's limited idea of kingship, which involves power used to force people and to control people. Jesus has changed the whole idea of kingship by becoming the Servant King, and the Suffering Servant at that. Our terms are too limited when it comes to describing the majesty of Jesus. A sad comment comes from the chief priests when they say, 'We have no king but the emperor.' Only too true, for they, like Pilate, have found it impossible to accept Jesus as their king and lord.

Have we allowed Christ to be our King? Do we seek to let him rule in our hearts and wills, or do we let other powers and events control our lives? Let us pray earnestly, 'Your kingdom come, your will be done in us as it is in heaven.'

Illustration

The school bus is at the top of a steep hill when the driver slumps at the wheel. The bus starts to swerve all over the road and is picking up speed. There is general panic on the bus for it is out of control. Two lads rush forward and move the driver off the seat. A girl grabs the steering wheel and gently applies the brakes. She has never driven before but knows what to do. One minute everything was out of control and the next the busload of children was rescued by the quick thinking and acting of three young people.

The world seems to have a tendency to run out of control; wars and rumours of wars, famine and earthquakes, violence and force seem to take over. Jesus warned us that these things would happen but that we should see them as the birth pangs of the new age, the coming of God's kingdom. We should celebrate that God is in control, that Christ is our Redeemer and King.